AMANDA CAHILL-RIPLEY

SOCIO-ECONOMIC RIGHTS IN TIMES OF CRISIS AND NORMALITY

Article 4 Limitations under the International Covenant on Economic, Social and Cultural Rights

BRISTOL
UNIVERSITY
PRESS

First published in Great Britain in 2025 by

Bristol University Press
University of Bristol
1–9 Old Park Hill
Bristol
BS2 8BB
UK
t: +44 (0)117 374 6645
e: bup-info@bristol.ac.uk

Details of international sales and distribution partners are available at
bristoluniversitypress.co.uk

British Library Cataloguing in Publication Data
A catalogue record for this book is available from the British Library

ISBN 978-1-5292-5177-7 hardcover
ISBN 978-1-5292-5178-4 ePub
ISBN 978-1-5292-5179-1 ePdf

Cover design: Blu inc
Front cover image: iStock/DrAfter123
Bristol University Press uses environmentally responsible print partners.
Printed and bound in Great Britain by CPI Group (UK) Ltd, Croydon, CR0 4YY

Bristol University Press' authorized representative in the European Union is: Easy Access System Europe, Mustamäe tee 50, 10621 Tallinn, Estonia,
Email: gpsr.requests@easproject.com

FSC
www.fsc.org
MIX
Paper | Supporting responsible forestry
FSC® C013604

This book is dedicated to my late friend and colleague Alison Graham

Contents

Acknowledgements

I would like to thank all of my colleagues and friends who have helped me on this journey. To the anonymous reviewers at Bristol University Press and the editorial team, especially Helen Davis and Grace Carroll. Special thanks to my trusty ESCRs colleagues especially Sigrun Skogly, Luke Graham and to all the ESRAN UKI members. Also, to the AHRI and Northern HRN; Professor Ludovic Hennebel; Geneva Academy of International Humanitarian Law and Human Rights, Lancaster University Law School, Amelia Susserott and, not least, the University of Liverpool School of Law and Social Justice and my SLSJ friends who have supported me – you know who you are! Thanks to Andreas Piperides for the WhatsApp and the inspiration, and finally thanks to the Gig Girls, my family and especially Tim, Fergus and Joe for their encouragement.

About the Author

Amanda Cahill-Ripley is Senior Lecturer in Law at the University of Liverpool School of Law and Social Justice, UK. She is also a Visiting Researcher at Lancaster University Law School, UK. She is an expert on international human rights law specialising in economic, social and cultural rights.

Table of Treaties

International Treaties

International Covenant on Civil and Political Rights 1966
International Covenant on Economic, Social and Cultural Rights 1966
Optional Protocol to the International Covenant on Economic, Social and Cultural Rights 2008
Vienna Convention on the Law of Treaties 1969

Regional Treaties

American Convention on Human Rights 1969
Additional Protocol to the American Convention on Human Rights in the Area of Economic, Social and Cultural Rights (Protocol of San Salvador) 1988
European Social Charter 1961
European Social Charter (Revised) 1996

Table of Cases

International Court of Justice

Legal Consequences of the Construction of a Wall in the Occupied Palestinian Territory, Advisory Opinion, I.C.J. Reports 2004, p 136.

Views Adopted by the Committee under the Optional Protocol to the International Covenant on Economic, Social and Cultural Rights

Views adopted by the Committee under the Optional Protocol to the International Covenant on Economic, Social and Cultural Rights, concerning Communications No. 226/2021 and No. 227/2021, *Hamid Saydawi and Masir Farah v Italy*, E/C.12/75/D/226/2021, E/C.12/75/D/227/2021 (13 March 2024).

Views adopted by the Committee under the Optional Protocol to the International Covenant on Economic, Social and Cultural Rights, concerning Communication No. 070/2018, *Sara Vázquez Guerreiro, D.S.V. and Y.S.V v Spain,* E/C.12/74/D/70/2018 (9 November 2023).

Views adopted by the Committee under the Optional Protocol to the International Covenant on Economic, Social and Cultural Rights, concerning Communication No. 061/2018, *Lorne Joseph Walters v Belgium*, E/C.12/70/D/61/2018 (23 November 2021).

Views adopted by the Committee under the Optional Protocol to the International Covenant on Economic, Social and Cultural Rights, concerning Communication No. 048/2018, *Romero and Children v Spain*, E/C.12/69/D/48/2018 (21 April 2021).

Views adopted by the Committee under the Optional Protocol to the International Covenant on Economic, Social and Cultural Rights, concerning Communication No. 054/2018, *El Ayoubi and Mohamed El Azouan Azouz v Spain*, E/C.12/69/D/54/2018 (23 March 2021).

Views adopted by the Committee under the Optional Protocol to the International Covenant on Economic, Social and Cultural Rights, concerning Communication No. 085/2018, *Hakima El Goumari and Ahmed Tidli v Spain*, E/C.12/69/D/85/2018 (16 March 2021).

Views adopted by the Committee under the Optional Protocol to the International Covenant on Economic, Social and Cultural Rights, concerning Communication No. 052/2018, *Gómez-Limón Pardo v Spain*, E/C.12/67/D/52/2018 (14 April 2020).

Views adopted by the Committee under the Optional Protocol to the International Covenant on Economic, Social and Cultural Rights, concerning Communication No. 037/2018, *López Albán v Spain*, E/C.12/66/D/37/2018 (29 November 2019).

Views adopted by the Committee under the Optional Protocol to the International Covenant on Economic, Social and Cultural Rights, concerning Communication No. 022/2017, *S.C. and G.P. v Italy*, E/C.12/65/D/22/2017 (28 March 2019).

Constitutional Courts

Government of the Republic of South Africa and Others v Grootboom and Others, 2001 (1) SA 46 (CC).

Introduction

Within the scholarly literature, the scope and application of article 4 of the International Covenant on Economic, Social and Cultural Rights 1966 (ICESCR),[1] has rarely been examined in any depth.[2] Further, there has been limited practice of the application of article 4 by relevant human rights bodies. 'While interference with civil and political rights is regularly examined, the extent to which states are allowed to restrict ESC rights is hardly ever raised.'[3] Moreover, the assumption is often made that article 4 limitations can only apply during a time of crisis or legal state of emergency, as opposed to contexts classified as 'normal' or 'peacetime'. In practice however, the contexts in which article 4 limitations can be invoked are more complex than this dichotomy suggests.

Due to the financial crisis of 2008 and the subsequent impacts of austerity measures on economic, social and cultural rights (ESCRs), some attention has been given to article 4 limitations (and their relationship to article 2(1) progressive realisation and retrogressive measures) in relation to *economic* crisis.[4] More

---

1 International Covenant on Economic, Social and Cultural Rights, adopted 1966. Entry into force 1976. Signatories: 71. Parties: 172. United Nations, Treaty Series, vol. 993, p 3.

2 As noted by Amrei Müller, 'Limitations to and Derogations from Economic, Social and Cultural Rights' (2009) 9(4) *Human Rights Law Review* 557, 558; Malcolm Langford, 'Chapter 8 Substantive Obligations' in Malcolm Langford, Bruce Porter, Rebecca Brown and Julieta Rossi (eds), *The Optional Protocol to the International Covenant on Economic, Social and Cultural Rights: A Commentary* (PULP 2016) 249.

3 Gilles Giacca, *Economic, Social, and Cultural Rights in Armed Conflict* (OUP 2014) 67–107, 67.

4 See Chapter Two.

recently due to the COVID-19 pandemic, limitations due to a *public health* emergency have been examined.[5] However, the application of article 4 within other crisis contexts, such as in a legal state of emergency or security crisis, natural disasters or in a conflict-affected situation (be it armed conflict, transition or post-conflict) has yet to be explored in theory. In addition, no systematic examination of article 4's application in practice (in times of crisis or peace) has been undertaken. Hence, this book aims to clarify the scope of permissible limitations that can be placed on ESCRs under the ICESCR. Further, it aims to elucidate the contexts in which such restrictions are applied, both in times of 'normality' and in times of 'crisis'.

Arguably, this book is needed now more than ever. With multiple crises facing the global community, understanding how human rights should apply in such contexts is crucial. In recent years, these multiple crises have intersected to challenge the enjoyment of ESCRs. Some have argued that these 'disparate crises interact such that the overall impact far exceeds the sum of each part',[6] forming a so-called 'poly-crisis'.[7] Others have argued that we are now in a permanent 'state of emergency' or crisis, such that any meaningful distinction can no longer be made between a state of normalcy and a state of crisis.[8] While questions concerning the broader theoretical debates around the existence and nature of a crisis (versus normality), are beyond the scope of this particular book,[9] what we can be certain of is that the combination of

5 See Chapter Two.

6 World Economic Forum, *The Global Risks Report 2023 18th Edition*, Insight Report (World Economic Forum: Geneva 2023) 9.

7 Adam Tooze, 'Welcome to the World of the Polycrisis', *Financial Times*, 28 October 2022, https://www.ft.com/content/498398e7-11b1-494b-9cd3-6d669dc3de33; World Economic Forum (n 6) 57.

8 Alan Greene, *Permanent States of Emergency and the Rule of Law: Constitutions in an Age of Crisis* (Hart Publishing, 2018).

9 For example, see Greene (n 8).

armed conflicts, the financial crisis and accompanying austerity measures, the COVID-19 pandemic and the climate crisis, 'combine to threaten profoundly the enjoyment of human rights, whether social, political, civil, economic, cultural or environmental in nature'.[10] Consequently, the contexts in which the enjoyment of ESCRs can lawfully be restricted need to be clear to prevent further deterioration in their enjoyment and/or violations.

Moreover, as Graham argues, the improved realisation of human rights, is conducive to greater resilience within society,[11] thus building resilience to economic, social, political and cultural crises. Consequently, 'when structural factors [...] reduce individual capacities to secure their rights [economic, social and cultural rights]',[12] the protection provided by the ICESCR is imperative. As such, now is the time to ensure the upmost protection and promotion of such rights and to scrutinise closely any limitations on ESCRs to ensure that are as in keeping with the provisions in the treaty.

Second, in terms of policy making at the international level, the United Nations (UN) Committee on Economic, Social and Cultural Rights (CESCR) is about to embark on drafting a new legal standard on the Application of the ICESCR in Situations of Armed Conflict.[13] This will require a clear framework for permissible limitations that can be applied in practice to ensure States Parties to the Covenant comply with their obligations in

[10] Aoife Nolan, 'Human rights and the cost-of-Living Crisis' (2023) 41(1) *Netherlands Quarterly of Human Rights* 3, 5.

[11] Luke David Graham, 'Poverty: The Cost-of-Living Perma-Crisis and the UDHR' (2024) 1 *European Human Rights Law Review* 31, 34.

[12] ibid 32.

[13] Closed-door Consultation on the General Comment of the Committee on Economic, Social and Cultural Rights on the Application of the International Covenant on Economic Social and Cultural Rights in Situations of Armed Conflict, Geneva Academy, Geneva (27 February 2025).

conflict-affected settings (CAS). In addition, the UN Special Rapporteur has called for input into his report on Economic, Social and Cultural Rights and Transitional Justice,[14] again highlighting the need to address the application of ESCRs in situations of crisis – in this case, transition. Consequently, the topicality, timeliness and relevance of this book for those in academia, policy and practice is clear.

The book does not consider the divergent limitations regimes under other international or regional human rights instruments.[15] Rather, the focus on the work of the UN CESCR is justified:

> because it is the only universal treaty body that has the role of monitoring the fulfilment of all ESCR in State parties all over the world. Thus, the CESCR has become a privileged forum for legal and policy discussions concerning ESCR and its doctrine has a special status, as it is the legal interpreter of the content of the ICESCR.[16]

---

14 Office of the United Nations High Commissioner for Human Rights, Special Procedures Branch, Expert meeting on 'Economic, Social and Cultural Rights in the Context of Transitional Justice' (21 February 2025).

15 In respect of ESCRs, of particular note but outside the scope of this book, are the provisions of Council of Europe, European Social Charter (18 October 1961) ETS 35, article 30 Derogations and article 31 Restrictions and the European Social Charter (Revised) (3 May 1996), ETS 163, Article G – Restrictions and Article F – Derogations in time of war or public emergency; Organisation of American States, Additional Protocol to the American Convention on Human Rights in the Area Of Economic, Social And Cultural Rights (Protocol of San Salvador), (17 November 1988), articles 4 and 5.

16 Rodrigo Uprimny, Sergio Chaparro Hernández and Andres Castro Araújo, 'Bridging the Gap: The Evolving Doctrine on ESCR and "Maximum Available Resources"' in Katherine Young (ed), *The Future of Economic and Social Rights. Globalization and Human Rights* (CUP 2019) 624, 626.

Neither does the book consider natural disasters or environmental crises, including the climate crisis.[17] This is because of the necessary limitations of scope but also due to the somewhat undeveloped nature of the application of ESCRs in relation to both disasters and environmental crises (which are ongoing, complex and have multiple facets).[18] The economic crisis, the pandemic and situations of armed conflict, provide discrete examples with a strong evidence base of the application of ESCRs, and some engagement around limitations on such rights under the ICESCR.

Chapter One examines the concept of limitations of human rights and traces the background and history of limitations clauses from the Universal Declaration of Human Rights (UDHR) to the drafting of the ICESCR. Building upon this historical scrutiny, it then provides a doctrinal analysis of the contemporary interpretation of article 4 under the ICESCR. Considering the *travaux préparatoires* and secondary literature to date, the chapter provides a doctrinal and theoretical understanding of the scope and content of restrictions that are permitted under the treaty, as well as identifying potential problems with the interpretation of article 4 to date including in relation to other key provisions under the treaty such as article 2(1).

Chapter Two examines how article 4 has been applied in practice, in various crises to date, and investigates the

[17] Although as Nolan highlights, there is a need for 'human rights bodies, policymakers and academics to engage meaningfully with the implications of shorter and longer-term responses to crises for the right to a safe, clean, healthy and sustainable environment'. See Nolan (n 10) 12.

[18] Such issues with regard to ESCRs are developing but are in their infancy. On the ICESCR in the context of disasters, see Stefanie Jansen-Wilhelm. *Accepting Assistance in the Aftermath of Disasters: Standards for States under International Law* (Intersentia 2015) especially Chapters 4 and 5.

reasons why States Parties to ICESCR might want to limit the enjoyment of economic and social rights. The chapter begins by considering the idea of emergency and crisis versus normality. In doing so, it examines the influence of the limitations regime under the International Covenant on Civil and Political Rights 1966 (ICCPR) and the legal question of derogations of human rights. The chapter subsequently examines three specific types of 'crises', namely the economic crisis, the public health crisis (COVID-19 pandemic) and situations of armed conflict (or conflict affected settings), to assess if and how article 4 has been engaged and to ascertain what lessons can be learnt if any from such experiences. Crucially, it is contended that there are areas of tension in the interpretation and use of article 4 to date, notably around the doctrine of progressive realisation and non-retrogression. Second, the strength of article 4 is that it can be invoked in times of normality, as well as in times of crisis, as it is not a derogation clause and does not trigger a legal state of emergency.

Chapter Three provides an overview and analysis of the use of article 4 by the UN human rights bodies, and States Parties to the ICESCR, based upon the findings of an original new primary empirical dataset. The empirical research undertaken consists of a deep dive textual analysis of over 400 UN documents using a combination of the Universal Human Rights Index (UHRI) database and gathering a new primary dataset using 'Atlas Ti' software. The subsequent sections offer in the first instance, a comprehensive overview of the practice of the UN CESCR regarding article 4 limitations in their standard setting (using General Comments and Statements), state monitoring process (Concluding Observations) and jurisprudence under the Optional Protocol to the International Covenant on Economic, Social and Cultural Rights 2008 individual communications process. Second, the chapter analyses the practice of the States Parties to ICESCR as reflected in their Periodic Reports to the Committee. Finally, a broader comparison is made with other relevant UN bodies practice concerning restrictions on ESCRs.[19] The purpose of this is to highlight the lack of consideration across the UN human rights system. The chapter closes with some critical reflections on the reasons for the findings.

Using the evidence gathered from both the doctrinal analysis and the empirical data, Chapter Four evaluates the existing legal framework for permissible limitations on economic, social and cultural rights under the ICESCR, noting the development of an increasingly complex conceptual framework with requirements additional to those explicitly provided within article 4 itself, notably the additional doctrines of *proportionality* and *reasonableness*. The chapter analyses the reasons for this evolution including the adoption of the Optional Protocol to the International Covenant on Economic, Social and Cultural Rights and the developing jurisprudence of the Committee, and considers the strengths and weaknesses of such an approach. It is contended that the addition of these further requirements to the framework for assessing limitations under the Covenant may actually provide too much flexibility as regards limitations on ESCRs, compounding the flexibility already provided for in article 4 alongside existing ICESCR doctrines found in article 2(1).

The final substantive chapter (Chapter Five), attempts to further delineate the parameters for clarifying the legal framework for article 4, providing a number of recommendations as to how best to develop a clear and consistent legal test for assessing article 4 limitations under the Covenant. Several key proposals are presented based around three central themes: first, clarity of scope and application; second, a call for specificity in terms of crisis and response; and third, that the limitations regime for ESCRs should be specific to such rights (due to their inherent nature) and should be in

[19] Universal Periodic Review and UN Special Procedures.

keeping with the authenticity and ethos of the Covenant and the *travaux préparatoires*. While presently, both theoretically and in practice, the concept of permissible limitations remains inconsistent and underdeveloped, by staying true to the primary concepts contained in the treaty, article 4 can be a useful and important provision supporting transparency, legitimacy and a lawful process for limiting ESCRs only when absolutely necessary.

The conclusion provides a summary of the key arguments made in the book and offers some brief concluding remarks.

ONE

The International Covenant on Economic, Social and Cultural Rights 1966, Article 4: A Doctrinal Analysis

In 1983 the UN Special Rapporteur of the Sub-Commission on Prevention of Discrimination and Protection of Minorities published a study on 'The Individual's Duties to the Community and the Limitations on Human Rights and Freedoms Under Article 29 of the Universal Declaration of Human Rights: A Contribution to the Freedom of the Individual Under Law'.[20] The study examined the question of permissible limitations on human rights under the UDHR but also under the two Covenants. UN member states, specialised agencies and regional organisations were invited to respond to a questionnaire on 'limitations on the exercise of human rights and fundamental freedoms'.[21] Further, the Special Rapporteur reviewed and considered the 'constitutional and

[20] Erica-Irene A. Daes, 'The Individual's Duties to the Community and the Limitations on Human Rights and Freedoms Under Article 29 of the Universal Declaration of Human Rights: A Contribution to the Freedom of the Individual Under Law'. Study prepared by Erica-Irene A. Daes, Special Rapporteur of the Sub-Commission on Prevention of Discrimination and Protection of Minorities, E/CN.4/Sub.2/432/Rev.2 (United Nations 1983).

[21] ibid 77–103, paras 96–8.

other provisions in selected States Members of the United Nations relating to limitations on the exercise of certain human rights and fundamental freedoms'.[22] Daes defined limitations on human rights as:

> Limitations or restrictions, [which] are placed not only on the exercise of certain rights of the individual but also on the power of the State to restrict the rights arbitrarily in any manner it might choose. This is the main purpose of, for example, the general limitations laid down in article 4 of the International Covenant on Economic, Social and Cultural Rights.[23]

The Special Rapporteur determined a number of basic principles, which 'should govern every limitation or restriction of or interference in the exercise of the rights or freedoms of the individual'.[24] These include, *inter alia*, the principle of legality, the principle of the rule of law, the principle of respect for the dignity of the individual and the principles of equality and non-discrimination.[25] Moreover, the Special Rapporteur considered that in addition to these basic principles, a number of other principles should be taken into account such as,

> (a) The principle of good faith;
> (b) The principle of respect for the acquired rights of the individual;
> (c) The principle of equity;
> (d) The principle of self-determination;
> (e) The principle of social solidarity, i.e., assistance by economically more advanced States or individuals to economically or socially weaker States or individuals;

[22] ibid 103–11, para. 99.
[23] ibid 69, para. 7.
[24] ibid 132–6, para. 354.
[25] ibid paras 355–75.

(f) The principle of friendly relations among peoples and States; and
(g) The principle of the maintenance of world peace.[26]

In examining these principles, it is clear that many of them are directly incorporated into the limitation regimes of the UDHR, the ICCPR and the ICESCR. More importantly however, several of these principles are a reminder of the key foundational values that should underpin the interpretation of limitations on human rights within all international and domestic law, namely respect for the dignity of the individual, non-discrimination and equity. In addition, certain principles would seem to hold special significance for economic social and cultural rights given their nature and resource questions, for example the principle of social solidarity. Such issues will be explored in due course. For now, it is prudent to examine how provisions for restrictions on economic and social rights developed within international human rights law and the resulting scope and content of the limitations clause under the ICESCR.

1.1 'Limiting human rights' under international human rights law – limitations under the UDHR

The drafting group for the International Bill of Human Rights was established in February 1947.[27] A preliminary draft was prepared by the Secretariat and was presented to the Committee at the first session. It contained 48 articles outlining

[26] ibid para. 394 (a)–(g).

[27] Established in accordance with a decision from the first session of the Commission on Human Rights (E/259). See also 27 March 1947 (E/383). See Universal Declaration of Human Rights (1948), Drafting History, Dag Hammarskjöld Library, Research Guides, Universal

individual human rights.[28] At this session, a working group was also established resulting in a report to the Commission on Human Rights that included drafts for an international declaration on Human Rights (Annex F) and draft articles to be considered for inclusion in a Convention (Annex G).[29] In its first form the provision on limitations, article 2 read as follows, 'In the exercise of his rights everyone is limited by the rights of others and by the just requirements of the State and of the United Nations.'[30]

By May 1948, in the second session of the Drafting Committee on International Bill of Human Rights,[31] there were various drafts and disagreement as to whether a limitations clause should be minimal or more extensive. Various proposals were put forward by states including *inter alia* recommendations from the USA, France and China.[32] The report on its second

Declaration of Human Rights (1948), Drafting History https://research.un.org/en/undhr/draftingcommittee

28 E/CN.4/AC.1/3, Draft Outline of International Bill of Rights. Universal Declaration of Human Rights (1948), Drafting History, Dag Hammarskjöld Library, Research Guides, Universal Declaration of Human Rights (1948), Drafting History, First Session. https://research.un.org/en/undhr/draftingcommittee/1

29 E/CN.4/21, ibid.

30 Commission on Human Rights, Drafting Committee on an International Bill of Human Rights, First Session, Report of the Drafting Committee to the Commission on Human Rights, E/CN.4/21 (1 July 1947) Annex A Commission on Human Rights, Report of the Drafting Committee on an International Bill of Human Rights, Draft Outline of an International Bill of Human Rights (Prepared by the Division of Human Rights of the Secretariat). https://docs.un.org/en/E/CN.4/21

31 Universal Declaration of Human Rights (1948), Drafting History, Dag Hammarskjöld Library, Research Guides, Universal Declaration of Human Rights (1948), Drafting History, Second Session 3 May–21 May 1948, New York. https://research.un.org/en/undhr/draftingcommittee/2

32 See US Recommendations E/CN.4/AC.1/20 (5 May 1948) Draft International Declaration on Human Rights (Document E/600)

session, E/CN.4/95, contained a redraft of article 2 under the revised Draft International Declaration of Human Rights (Annex A)[33] which stated:

> Article 2 (The Drafting Committee did not have time to consider this Article) In the exercise of his rights everyone is limited by the rights of others and by the just requirements of the democratic State. The individual owes duties to society through which he is enabled to develop his spirit, mind and body in wider freedom.[34]

However, the Committee noted that they did not have time to consider this article. Consequently, it was at the Third Session of the Commission on Human Rights that the draft individual articles and the declaration as a whole was revised and adopted. The re-drafted Declaration was adopted by the Commission on Friday 18 June 1948, with 12 votes in favour, none against and 4 abstentions.[35] In Annex A of the Draft Declaration the limitations clause had developed to include specific requirements enabling limitations:

---

with United States' Recommendations, p. 1502; French Government Observations E/CN.4/82/Add.8 (6 May 1948) Original Text: French Observations of Governments on the Draft International Declaration on Human Rights, the Draft International Covenant on Human Rights, and Methods of Application Communication Received from the French Government, p. 1649; Chinese amendments to draft article 2 – China E/CN.4/102 (27 May 1948) China: Amendments to the Draft International Declaration on Human Rights, in William Schabas (ed), *The Universal Declaration of Human Rights: The Travaux Préparatoires* (CUP 2013) 1493.

[33] See Economic and Social Council, E/CN.4/95 (21 May 1948), Commission on Human Rights Drafting Committee, Second Session, Annex A, https://documents.un.org/doc/undoc/gen/gl9/001/66/pdf/gl900166.pdf

[34] ibid article 2.

[35] E/CN.4/SR.81 in Schabas (n 32) 1697.

Article 27

1. Everyone has duties to the community, which enables him freely to develop his personality.
2. In the exercise of his rights, everyone shall be subject only to such limitations as are necessary to secure due recognition and respect for the rights of others and the requirements of morality, public order and general welfare in a democratic society.[36]

Further by the beginning of the December session of 1948, the text of article 27 as adopted by the Sub-Committee of the Third Committee read as follows:

Article 27

1. Everyone has duties to the community in which alone the free and full development of his personality is possible.
2. In the exercise of his rights and freedoms, everyone shall be subject only to such limitations as are prescribed by law solely for the purpose of securing due recognition and respect for the rights and freedoms of others and of meeting the just requirements of morality, public order and the general welfare in a democratic society.
3. Those rights and freedoms may in no case be exercised contrary to the purpose and principles of the United Nations.[37]

In its final draft form, the draft Universal Declaration of Human Rights consisted of a preamble and 31 articles that were put

[36] Annex A Draft International Declaration of Human Rights, Report of the Third Session of the Commission on Human Rights, Lake Success, 24 May to 18 June 1948 E/800 (28 June 1948) in Schabas (n 32) 1973.

[37] A/C.3/SC.4/20 (3 December 1948), Text of Articles of the Draft Declaration as Adopted by the Sub-Committee 4, Third Committee, in Schabas (n 32) 2944, 2939.

to the vote article by article. Article 27 became article 29 and read as follows:

> Article 29: Duties and Limitations
> 1. Everyone has duties to the community in which alone the free and full development of his personality is possible.
> 2. In the exercise of his rights and freedoms, everyone shall be subject only to such limitations as are determined by law solely for the purpose of securing due recognition and respect for the rights and freedoms of others and of meeting the just requirements of morality, public order and the general welfare in a democratic society.
> 3. These rights and freedoms may in no case be exercised contrary to the purposes and principles of the United Nations.

In the General Assembly vote on the text proposed by the Third Committee, article 29 was adopted by 47 votes, with 8 abstentions.[38] The draft UDHR as a whole was then put to the vote by roll call and was adopted by 48 votes, with 8 abstentions.[39]

As Opsahl notes, it is interesting that even in the non-binding 'common standard of achievement' of the UDHR it was felt necessary to include a limitations provision.[40] It is also interesting that even at this early stage the question as to the scope and extent of limitations caused some discussion and disagreement between members of the drafting committee.[41]

---

[38] See A/PV.183169 (10 December 1948), Official Records of the General Assembly, Third Session, pp 912–35 in Schabas (n 32) 3089.

[39] ibid.

[40] Torkel Opsahl, 'Articles 29 and 30: The Other Side of the Coin' in Asbjørn Eide (ed), *The Universal Declaration of Human Rights: A Commentary* (Scandinavian University Press, 1992) 449.

[41] For example, cf article 2 of the Secretariat, E/CN.4/AC.1/11 (12 June 1947) with US Proposals, E/CN.4/AC.1/8 (11 June 1947); 'The state is created by the people for the promotion of their welfare and the protection of their mutual rights. In the exercise of his rights everyone is

Looking at article 29, it is evident that elements were subsequently incorporated into both article 4 of the ICCPR and article 4 of the ICESCR. However, notably this provision applied to all rights, civil and political, and economic, social and cultural. As such, the requirements set out in article 29(2) were selectively incorporated into each Covenant. Further, 'the provision for duties was removed from the binding provisions of the covenants to the Preambles'.[42] Concerning limitations the UDHR specifically refers 'only to the exercise of rights, thus implying, perhaps, for instance that the rights themselves cannot be limited in substance. But it is submitted that there is no real difference between the substance and the exercise of a right'.[43]

1.2 Drafting the limitations clause for the proposed Covenant on Human Rights – insights from the *travaux préparatoires*

The history of the drafting of the limitations clause under the UDHR was significant because it informed the drafting of the limitations clause during the preparatory negotiations for the proposed human rights Covenant, which subsequently became the ICESCR and the ICCPR. It is evident that the text of the UDHR article 29 helped to shape the final adopted clause provided in ICESCR as illustrated by the *travaux préparatoires*. In May 1951, during the Commission on Human Rights 7th Session on the 'Draft International Covenant on Human Rights and Methods of Implementation', the US proposed a general limitations clause, which read as follows:

> Each State Party to the Covenant recognises that in the enjoyment of those rights provided by the State in

limited by the rights of others. The state may impose only such limitations on such rights as are compatible with the freedom and welfare of all,' in Schabas (n 32) 748.

42 Opsahl (n 40) 454.

43 ibid 460.

> conformity with this Part of the Covenant, the State may subject such rights only to such limitations as are determined by law and solely for the purpose of securing due recognition and respect for the rights and freedoms of others and of meeting the just requirements of morality, public order and the general welfare in a democratic society.[44]

In the July sessions of the Commission, discussion ensued as to whether a general limitations clause was required for the section on ESCRs within (as it was at this point) the joint draft Covenant.[45] The Chairman of the Commission pointed out that the US proposal for limitations was drafted along the lines of existing limitation clauses in articles 13, 14, 15 and 16 of Part II of the [draft] covenant. 'While admitting the importance of a general limitation clause, he felt the adoption of a proposal such as that submitted by the US delegation might seriously restrict the applicability of certain of the articles relating to economic, social and cultural rights already adopted.'[46] Mrs Roosevelt, representative for the USA, referred to UDHR article 29 as the foundation for the USA proposal on a general limitations clause, noting that 'The US delegation proposed the inclusion in the part of

---

[44] Commission on Human Rights 7th Session, Agenda Item 3(b) on the Draft International Covenant on Human Rights and Methods of Implementation, 'USA: Proposal Relating to a General Clause Concerning Economic, Social and Cultural Rights, E/CN.4/610/Add.2 (5 May 1951)' in Ben Saul (ed) *The International Covenant on Economic, Social and Cultural Rights: Travaux Préparatoires, Volume I* (OUP 2016) 722.

[45] See Commission on Human Rights 7th Session, 'Agenda Item 3(b) on the Draft International Covenant on Human Rights and Methods of Implementation', Meetings 234–6 (2 July 1951), in Saul (n 44) 553–5.

[46] Commission on Human Rights 7th Session, Agenda Item 3(b) on the Draft International Covenant on Human Rights and Methods of Implementation, '234th Meeting, E/CN.4/SR.234 (2 July 1951)', in Saul (n 44) 553.

the Covenant dealing with economic, social and cultural rights of a general recognition that the rights, when provided by the State, would not necessarily be absolute, but might be subject to the limitations mentioned in article 29 of the UDHR.'[47]

Uruguay suggested amendments to shorten the proposed provision, questioning whether the clause needed to 'provide for as many limitations as were foreseen in the USA proposal'.[48] They argued that the proposal was too broad and the expressions 'just requirements of morality', 'public order' and 'general welfare' were difficult to interpret.[49] Uruguay therefore proposed a single limitation:

> Each State Party to the Covenant recognises that in the enjoyment of those rights provided by the State in conformity with this Part of the Covenant, the State may subject such rights only to such limitations as may be determined by law in the interests of the community in a democratic society.[50]

The USA said it was prepared to accept the amendment.[51] Lebanon also proposed shortening the USA proposal and suggested replacing the last three lines with 'and solely for the purpose of promoting the general welfare in a democratic society'.[52] This amendment was also supported by the USA.[53]

---

47 Commission on Human Rights 7th Session, Agenda Item 3(b) on the Draft International Covenant on Human Rights and Methods of Implementation, '234th Meeting, E/CN.4/SR.234 (2 July 1951)', in Saul (n 44) 554.

48 ibid.

49 ibid.

50 ibid.

51 ibid.

52 Commission on Human Rights 7th Session, Agenda Item 3(b) on the Draft International Covenant on Human Rights and Methods of Implementation, '235th Meeting, E/CN.4/SR.235 (2 July 1951)', in Saul (n 44) 555.

53 ibid 561.

Overall arguments in support of adopting a specific limitations clause for ESCRs were made by representatives of France, Australia and Greece.[54] Yugoslavia, Chile, Soviet Union and the Ukrainian Soviet Socialist Republic (SSR) made arguments against the adoption of a specific clause.[55] Yugoslavia highlighted that article 29 of the UDHR applied to all rights, civil and political rights (CPR) and ESCRs. As such it was not clear why such an equivalent clause should be applied specifically and solely to ESCRs.[56] India stated they did not think there was need for a limitation clause 'of the kind submitted by the USA delegation covering economic, social and cultural rights, as there was in the case of civil and political rights', with the representative asking 'how the enjoyment of rights such as health, education and working conditions could be limited'.[57]

Interestingly, Pakistan argued that the USA proposal:

> was more relevant to civil and political rights than to economic, social and cultural rights [...] A general limitation clause would [...] tend to curtail the enjoyment of those rights [...]. Inequalities in the application of economic, social and cultural rights lay at the root of all degradation and frustration. Limitation should therefore be conceived in terms of adjustment, not in those of curtailment.[58]

This argument would seem to 'pave the way' for the notion of progressive realisation and priority for vulnerable groups as now contained in the ICESCR. Denmark abstained from voting on the proposal. China supported the USA proposal if

---

[54] ibid 555–65.

[55] ibid.

[56] ibid 565.

[57] ibid 555.

[58] ibid 562.

specific qualifying clauses for specific rights (such as the right to work) were removed.[59]

The final amended clause was adopted by 11 votes to 6 with one abstention as follows:

> Each State Party to the Covenant recognises that in the enjoyment of those rights provided by the State in conformity with this Part of the Covenant, the State may subject such rights only to such limitations as are determined by law only insofar as this may be compatible with the nature of these rights, and solely for the purpose of promoting the general welfare in a democratic society.[60]

This included the Chilean amendment to insert 'only insofar as this may be compatible with the nature of these rights'[61] and the Uruguayan amendment changing the word 'interest' to 'welfare'.[62] This draft provision initially adopted as article 32 of the Draft Covenant on Human Rights[63] became article 4 of the Draft Covenant on ESCRs, which was subsequently adopted at the 8th session of the Commission in 1952.[64]

When the text of the draft covenants was discussed at the General Assembly in 1955, the question of limitations was

---

59 ibid 555–65.

60 Commission on Human Rights 7th Session, Agenda Item 3(b) on the Draft International Covenant on Human Rights and Methods of Implementation, '236th Meeting, E/CN.4/SR.236 (2 July 1951)', in Saul (n 44) 565–71, 571.

61 ibid 569.

62 ibid 570.

63 See article 32 of Draft Covenant prepared at the seventh session E/1952, Annex I. See 'Report to the Economic and Social Council on the Eighth Session of the Commission, E/2256; E/CN.4/669 (14 April 1952–14 June 1952)' in Saul (n 44) 1268–98, 1295.

64 Annex I Draft International Covenants on Human Rights and Measures of Implementation – A Draft Covenant on ESCRs, Text of provisions

revisited. Now the draft covenants had been split, discussions centred around whether the draft article 4 was sufficient[65] and specifically how a general limitations clause would work alongside the now draft article 2 of ICESCR.[66] Those remaining opposed to article 4 or to its expansion contended that:

> an article on general limitations was superfluous, since the provisions of the draft International Covenant on Economic, Social and Cultural Rights were already limited by article 2 of that covenant. General limitations would be open to varying interpretations and would tend to weaken or destroy the binding force of the provisions of the covenant. [...] The nature of the obligations imposed and the manner of enunciating the rights made limitations generally unnecessary.[67]

However, those who supported article 4 stressed the fact that:

> the provisions of article 2 should relate only to the general level of attainment of rights and should not be invoked by states as grounds for imposing numerous limitations on them. Article 2 did not indicate when limitations should be legitimate and it was necessary to state clearly that limitations would be permissible only in certain circumstances and under certain conditions.[68]

---

adopted at the 8th session of the Commission, article 4. Text as per adopted treaty (previously article 32 of Draft Covenant prepared at the seventh session E/1952, Annex I).

65 'Annotations on the Text of the Draft International Covenants on Human Rights (Prepared by the Secretary-General), A/2929 (1 July 1955)', in Ben Saul (ed) *The International Covenant on Economic, Social and Cultural Rights: Travaux Preparatoires, Volume II* (OUP 2016) 1533–96, 1562, para. 48.

66 ibid 1563, paras 49–50.

67 ibid 1563, para. 49.

68 ibid para. 50.

Other concerns were raised regarding the different nature of CPRs vis-à-vis ESCRs, contending that 'It was not feasible to treat economic, social and cultural rights in the same way [as civil and political rights] since the manner in which the articles were drafted was different.'[69] Moreover, that such a difference ensured that 'Such considerations as morality, public order and the rights and freedoms of others were more relevant to civil and political rights than to economic, social and cultural rights' (and rights and freedoms of others covered in article 5(1) anyway).[70]

Moving forwards in what was a slow and arduous process, some seven years later, when reflecting on the text of the draft article, a number of observations and criticisms were raised by the States Parties in the General Assembly meeting in November 1962: Indonesia contended that the phrase 'compatible with the nature of these rights' was unclear and open to different interpretations. They argued it might be interpreted as meaning some rights that could not be limited at all due to their very nature, or that all rights in the Covenant could be subject to limitations. They recommended deletion of the phrase.[71] Likewise, Cuba noted that this phrase was too vague.[72]

Brazil asserted that the text of article 4 was generally 'ambiguous', 'vague and imprecise' and that the text 'weakened the covenant' and should be redrafted. In relation to the specific phrase, 'general welfare in a democratic society' they maintained that due to the 'diversity of opinions concerning what was meant by democratic society' such a provision 'was quite useless'.[73] Pakistan also questioned this phrase, insisting

---

69 ibid para. 51.

70 ibid para. 52.

71 General Assembly, 17th session, 1184th Meeting, A/C.3/SR.1184 (15 November 1962), in Saul (n 65) 2166–75, 2171, para. 43.

72 General Assembly, 17th session, 1185th Meeting, A/C.3/SR.1185 (16 November 1962) in Saul (n 65) 2175–85, 2179, para. 26.

73 General Assembly, A/C.3/SR.1184 (15 November 1962) (n 71) 2173, para. 49.

that it would only be acceptable 'on the understanding that the expression "the general welfare" included State security. It was out of the question to promote the general welfare at the expense of collective security.'[74] Pakistan also argued for 'widest possible interpretation' of 'in a democratic society'.[75]

Finally, in December of 1962, 'Article 4 as a whole, as proposed by the Commission on Human Rights, was adopted unanimously.'[76] While some states thought the phrases 'compatible with nature of rights' and 'in a democratic society', 'might give rise to difficulties of interpretation', it was felt overall that the clause 'adequately expressed the essential idea that arbitrary limitation of the rights recognised in the draft Covenant could not be allowed'.[77]

From this analysis of the *travaux préparatoires*, we can ascertain a number of important points; first, that there was some dissatisfaction with the general limitations clause even though it was adopted unanimously. Second, despite evidence of 'some confusion about the concepts of, and relationship between, progressive realization and the limitation of rights',[78] it was always the intention of the States Parties to differentiate between article 2(1) which would apply to resource issues and article 4 which would apply to other types of limitations. As Saul et al note, 'the principles [...] apply concurrently and on different conceptual planes'.[79] This is also reflected in the fact that article 8 on the right to form and join trade unions was

74 General Assembly, A/C.3/SR.1185 (16 November 1962) (n 72) 2184, para. 54.

75 ibid.

76 General Assembly, 17th Session, Agenda Item 43, Report of the Third Committee A/5365 (17 December 1962) in Saul (n 65) 2230, para. 91.

77 ibid 2230, para. 89.

78 Ben Saul, David Kinley and Jacqueline Mowbray, *The International Covenant on Economic, Social and Cultural Rights: Commentary, Cases, and Materials* (OUP 2014) 247.

79 ibid.

drafted with a specific limitations clause because it was felt it did not engage resource issues.[80] On reflection, it is perhaps as a result of this unresolved underlying disquiet and lack of agreement over the scope and content of article 4 that still underpins the difficulties in interpreting and applying article 4 today.

1.3 Limitations under the ICESCR – Doctrinal interpretation of article 4 ICESCR

The general limitations clause is provided for in article 4 of the ICESCR:

> The States Parties to the present Covenant recognise that, in the enjoyment of those rights provided by the State in conformity with the present Covenant, the State may subject such rights only to such limitations as are *determined by law* only in so far as this may be *compatible with the nature of these rights* and solely for the purpose of promoting the *general welfare in a democratic society*.[81]

This general provision applies to all of the substantive rights within Part III of the covenant with the exception of Part I, article 1, the right to self-determination.[82] As noted previously, none of the rights contained within ICESCR are subject to right specific limitations with the sole exception of article 8 trade union rights.[83] However, article 4 is supported by

80 General Assembly, 11th Session, Third Committee, 721st Meeting, A/C.3/SR.721 (4 January 1957), in Saul (n 65) 1782–8, 1785. paras 19–21 (Lebanon).

81 International Covenant on Economic, Social and Cultural Rights 1966, article 4. Emphasis added.

82 Philip Alston and Gerard Quinn, 'The Nature and Scope of States Parties' Obligations under the International Covenant on Economic, Social and Cultural Rights' (1987) 9(2) *Human Rights Quarterly* 156, 192.

83 ibid.

a 'savings clause',[84] article 5(1), which provides a further constraint on any limitations permitted under the ICESCR:

> Nothing in the present Covenant may be interpreted as implying for any State, group or person any right to engage in any activity or to perform any act aimed at the destruction of any of the rights or freedoms recognized herein, *or at their limitation to a greater extent than is provided for in the present Covenant.*[85]

This 'interpretative rule [...] prohibits any unreasonable interpretation of the limitations on human rights envisaged in, [...], articles 4 and 8 of the International Covenant on Economic, Social and Cultural Rights'.[86] Together, article 4 supported by article 5 in a subsidiary role,[87] form the basis for limitations under the ICESCR.[88]

As Saul notes, 'the central purpose of article 4 is to ensure that states must not arbitrarily limit ICESCR rights'.[89] Alston and Quinn note the dual function of article 4: it is both permissive in that it permits states to impose limitations on the enjoyment of Covenant rights, but it is also protective in that it limits 'the purposes for which limitations may be imposed and the manner

---

84 Lisa Forman, 'The Evolving International Law Standards Governing Restrictions of Economic, Social and Cultural Rights during Public Emergencies' (2024) 1(2) *Journal of Global Health Law* 177, 182.

85 ICESCR article 5(1). Emphasis added.

86 Daes (n 20) 69, para. 10.

87 Saul, Kinley and Mowbray (n 78) 266. Further discussion of article 5 is outside the scope of this book. However, it is notable that it, too, has been subject to little scrutiny in theory and practice.

88 Magdalena Sepúlveda, *The Nature of the Obligations Under the International Covenant on Economic, Social, and Cultural Rights* (Intersentia 2003) 305.

89 Saul, Kinley and Mowbray (n 78) 242; Committee on Human Rights, Report to ECOSOC, E/2256 (supp) (1 January 1952), 24; UNGA Third Committee A/5365 (17 December 1962), 24; Daes (n 20) 69, para. 7.

in which that may be legitimately done'.[90] Consequently, in essence article 4 sets out a triple test for determining legitimate limitations on ESCRs. Such limitations must be:

1. Determined by law;
2. Compatible with the nature of these rights;
3. For the purpose of promoting general welfare in a democratic society.[91]

Moreover, the Limburg Principles on the Implementation of the International Covenant on Economic, Social and Cultural Rights state, 'Article 4 was intended to be protective of the rights of individuals rather than permissive of the imposition of limitations by the state.'[92] Thus, the onus is on the state to meet the triple test if they wish or need to restrict ESCRs.

1.3.1 'Determined by law'

The phrase 'as are determined by law', is taken directly from article 29(2) the UDHR. Daes explains that

> human rights [...] although protected by the Universal Declaration of Human Rights and secured by the International Covenants on Human Rights, must be exercised in accordance with the law of the State. However, that law and its application must not be such as to be contrary to the purpose and the spirit of those international instruments.[93]

---

90 Alston and Quinn (n 82) 193.

91 NB Article 4 does not explicitly mention 'legitimate aims' or 'proportionality'.

92 Limburg Principles on the Implementation of the International Covenant on Economic, Social and Cultural Rights E/CN.4/1987/17 (8 January 1987), article 4, para. 46.

93 Daes (n 20) 112, para. 127.

Evidently, 'That law must be just, otherwise it would be interpreted as authorizing States to impose any limitations or restrictions they wished.'[94] Consequently, the phrase *determined by law*, must be qualified. Otherwise, it 'would mean in effect that the State would be able to avoid its international obligations in the matter by enacting laws limiting the individual's rights and freedoms'.[95]

Further guidance on the interpretation of these specific 'protective' phrases can also be taken from the Limburg Principles, paras 48–51, which provide an interpretation of the requirement for limitations to be '*determined by law*',

> 48. No limitation on the exercise of economic, social and cultural rights shall be made unless provided for by national law of general application, which is consistent with the Covenant and is in force at the time the limitation is applied.
>
> 49. Laws imposing limitations on the exercise of economic, social and cultural rights shall not be arbitrary or unreasonable or discriminatory.
>
> 50. Legal rules limiting the exercise of economic, social and cultural rights shall be clear and accessible to everyone.
>
> 51. Adequate safeguards and effective remedies shall be provided by law against illegal or abusive imposition on application of limitations on economic, social and cultural rights.[96]

As noted previously, the concept of lawful restrictions then also includes the underlying principle of non-discrimination

---

[94] ibid para. 128.

[95] ibid para. 129.

[96] Limburg Principles (n 92) paras 48–51.

and thus protects a vulnerable or marginalised group from unreasonable or discriminatory application of limitations.[97] However, no further detail is provided as to what would constitute 'unreasonable'.[98]

Alston and Quinn note that in determining the meaning of this phrase, inspiration can be also be drawn from similar clauses and jurisprudence under other international human rights treaties such as the European Convention on Human Rights, and The Siracusa Principles on the Limitation and Derogation Provisions in the International Covenant on Civil and Political Rights.[99] Consequently, this clause can be interpreted to include 'what form the law must take, how much discretion the law gives to authorities [and] the requirement that the restriction be accessible and foreseeable'.[100]

1.3.2 'Compatible with the nature of these rights'

The protective clause, '"*compatible with the nature of these rights*" requires that a limitation shall not be interpreted or applied so as to jeopardize the essence of the right concerned'.[101] This restriction ensures that all limitations must be considered in light of each specific right within the Covenant. As such, there may be some rights that cannot be subject to any limitations

97 Limburg Principles (n 92) para. 49.

98 The idea of whether such limitations are 'unreasonable' is explored in Chapter Four in relation to the developing jurisprudence of the CESCR which contributes to understanding this point.

99 For example, the Limburg Principles 48–51 are derived from the International Commission of Jurists, Siracusa Principles on the Limitation and Derogation Provisions in the International Covenant on Civil and Political Rights (1985) Principles 15–18, United Nations Doc. E/CN.4/1984/4 (28 September 1984). https://www.icj.org/wp-content/uploads/1984/07/Siracusa-principles-ICCPR-legal-submission-1985-eng.pdf

100 Alston and Quinn (n 82) 200. See also Limburg Principles (n 92) 50.

101 ibid para. 56.

under article 4 if the very nature of those rights is considered (they may still be subject to article 2(1) resource limitations). For example, 'it is difficult to see how the right to freedom from hunger (article 11) could be subject to limitations that would not be inconsistent with its very nature (except on article 2(1) grounds)'.[102]

1.3.3 'General welfare'

Notably, it is only within the UDHR and ICESCR that *general welfare* constitutes a ground for imposing limitations on human rights.[103] Daes quoting *Black's Law Dictionary* defines 'welfare' as 'well-doing or well-being in any respect; and enjoyment of health and common blessings of life'.[104] In the context of limitations, the meaning of the phrase 'solely for the purpose of promoting the general welfare in a democratic society' within article 4 is taken directly from article 29(2) of the UDHR. Significantly, it can be understood in this context to have a narrower interpretation, as it is not accompanied by the other 'just requirements' included within article 29(2) UDHR, that is, maintenance of morality and public order. As Alston and Quinn note, 'while considerations of public order and morality might justify limitations on civil and political rights, they do not seem to be relevant in the same sense with respect to limitations on economic, social and cultural rights'.[105]

The idea of 'general welfare' 'varies with the time and the state of society and its needs'.[106] Thus, it is a flexible concept that can account for 'circumstances prevailing at a particular time'.[107] Yet, it always encompasses a utilitarian, communal element.

---

102 Alston and Quinn (n 82) 201.
103 Daes (n 20) 176, para. 1010.
104 Daes (n 20) 123, para. 254.
105 Alston and Quinn (n 82) 202.
106 Daes (n 20) 176, para. 1012.
107 ibid 176, para. 1013.

Daes' study noted that 'Since man identifies himself with his community, he must yield priority to the general welfare, in so far as this is compatible with his human dignity.'[108] In other words, sometimes an individual right must be restricted for the good of the greater society. Moreover, 'The measure of the public interest should define the extent of restriction of the individual's freedom.'[109]

This understanding of the general welfare can also be found in the Limburg Principles where the phrase is interpreted as meaning 'furthering the well-being of the people as a whole'.[110] It is also notable that, in practice, the term has also been used interchangeably with the phrase 'promoting the "common good" in a democratic society'. Thus, the CESCR has interpreted the term *general welfare* as synonymous with 'common good' of the people.[111] Somewhat self-evidently, the phrase 'solely for the purpose' ensures that, national legislative and administrative bodies can only limit economic, social and cultural rights on grounds explicitly provided by article 4 ICESCR.[112]

1.3.4 'In a democratic society'

'The term "democracy" has a long history and has been applied with some consistency to a form of government in which the "demos", the people, rule, i.e. in which the political

108 ibid 123, para. 252.

109 ibid 176, para. 1020.

110 Limburg Principles (n 92) 52.

111 For example, in CESCR Communication No. 54/2018 *El Ayoubi and Mohamed El Azouan Azouz* v. *Spain*, E/C.12/69/D/54/2018 (23 March 2021), para. 11.3, 'Thus, in order for an eviction to be justifiable, it must meet the following requirements: firstly, the limitation must be determined by law; secondly, it must promote the common good in a democratic society.'

112 Daes (n 20) 124, para. 265. See also 178, para. 1049.

power is held by the many rather than by the one or the few.'[113] While there are many types of democracies,[114] Daes argues that they 'are only real and pure democracies when they guarantee and respect human rights and fundamental freedoms'.[115] In the context of the ICESCR, the meaning of the phrase 'democratic society' can be interpreted to mean, a society that respects the principles of the UN Charter and the UDHR. Such an interpretation was central to avoiding ideological and political debates at the time of drafting.[116] This interpretation is also reflected in the Siracusa Principles and the Limburg Principles on the Implementation of the International Covenant on Economic, Social and Cultural Rights, the latter of which states, 'While there is no single model of a democratic society, a society which recognizes and respects the human rights set forth in the United Nations Charter and the Universal Declaration of Human Rights may be viewed as meeting this definition.'[117] Moreover, within the Limburg Principles, the expression 'in a democratic society' is understood as 'imposing a further restriction on the application of limitations',[118] with, 'The burden is upon a State imposing limitations, to demonstrate that the limitations do not impair the democratic functioning of the society.'[119]

1.4 Concluding remarks

In conclusion, it is evident that since the inception of the UDHR to the adoption of the ICESCR the subject of permissible limitations has been contentious and debated,

[113] ibid 127, para. 298.
[114] ibid 128, para. 313.
[115] ibid 128, para. 314.
[116] Alston and Quinn (n 82) 203.
[117] Limburg Principles (n 92) 55.
[118] ibid 53.
[119] ibid 54.

with arguments for both narrow and broad limitations clauses. The adopted legal texts on limitations under both the UDHR and the ICESCR were a result of compromise and likely time restraints. However, a number of points are clear: first, as a general rule, 'provisions providing for limitations should be interpreted narrowly'.[120] Even the adopted text of the UDHR illustrates that finding consensus on the wording for a provision even within a non-binding declaration was a long drawn-out process. However, the relatively narrow grounds for permissible restrictions under the UDHR is quite remarkable given that it is applicable to all human rights, CPRs and ESCRs.

Second, concerning limitations under the ICESCR, it is clear that there was some disagreement on the need for a general limitations clause within the ICESCR. The nexus between article 2 and the inherent 'limitations' it provides through its provision for progressive realisation and maximum available resources, were considered by some to provide sufficient constraints on ESCRs. This 'muddiness' between article 2(1) and article 4 remains to this day and may be one reason why article 4 has been misinterpreted or under-utilised in practice.

Significantly, despite arguments to further align article 4 with provisions in the draft ICCPR, the resulting article 4 is intentionally specific to ESCRs and narrow in scope. As Alston and Quinn note, 'the pre-eminent concern of the drafters of article 4 was to ensure that limitations could not lightly be justified'.[121]

Keeping this in mind and having examined the historical and doctrinal aspects of article 4, the subsequent question to consider is how article 4 has been interpreted and applied to date. The following chapter considers the situations in which article 4 has been invoked to date.

[120] Daes (n 20) 172, para. 929.

[121] Alston and Quinn (n 82) 202.

TWO

Why Do States Invoke Article 4 to Limit ESCRs? ESCRs in Times of Crisis and Normality

Given the requirements of article 4 and the triple test that must be satisfied for such limitations to be permissible, why then and in what circumstances do states invoke article 4 limitations? Legally, as evidenced previously, no emergency or crisis is required for states to employ article 4. However, in practice it would appear logical that States Parties will utilise article 4 when faced with a situation that they deem different from the norm – challenging for the implementation of economic, social and cultural rights. It is also true, however, that the question of whether the nature of the 'emergency' or crisis should or does make a difference to how article 4 is applied is not one which has been considered in any depth. In examining how article 4 has been applied previously, until the advent of the financial crisis and austerity measures in 2008, article 4 had been rarely invoked by states or indeed interpreted by the CESCR. More recently, article 4 limitations have been discussed in the context of the COVID-19 global pandemic, but it is argued that each of these 'crises' or 'emergencies' raise different and specific challenges for limitations of ESCRs. Moreover, should a state of emergency or crisis make any difference to how article 4 is applied, given the ICESCR does not provide for any specific emergency regime.

Consequently, this chapter will examine concepts of emergency and crisis in relation to their impacts on the application of ESCRs. It will explore the legal implications of classifying a situation a 'state of emergency', as opposed to a crisis, and consider whether there are any grounds under which ESCRs can be derogated from such as in a public emergency. It will subsequently explore how article 4 has been applied in other specific situations deemed 'crises' to date, including the economic crisis, the health crisis caused by COVID-19 and the question of armed conflict and natural disasters as crises. By analysing such previous experiences, information as to if, and how, article 4 has been applied can be obtained, and commonalities and divergences in practice identified.

2.1 Crisis, state of emergency and the ICESCR

As noted in the Introduction, the question of whether the current global state of affairs can be characterised as a permanent state of crisis, a poly-crisis or indeed normality is a matter of ongoing debate. What is crucial, however, is to determine what we mean by the terms crisis or emergency when examining the application of ICESCR in such contexts and the impacts these situations have on economic and social rights enjoyment. Are the terms 'crisis' and 'emergency' synonymous? Do they engage the same legal regimes and responses?

Greene defines a 'state of emergency' as, 'a crisis identified and labelled by a state to be of such magnitude that it is deemed to cross a threat severity threshold, necessitating urgent, exceptional and, consequently, temporary actions by the state not permissible when normal conditions exist'.[122] This definition indicates that a state of emergency is more than a crisis – it is, in fact, an extreme form of crisis. As Greene

[122] Greene (n 8) 30; xiv.

contends, an emergency can be characterised as a crisis of 'extreme magnitude and urgency'.[123]

Such 'states of emergency' are recognised and provided for in international and domestic legal systems across the world,[124] in recognition that such exceptional situations require 'novel legal norms' as a response. The rationale for this is that the 'existing legal powers and legal order are insufficient to deal with the events at hand'.[125] As such, the legal concept of a 'state of emergency' and the corresponding legal tools to enable such an emergency paradigm, that is, derogations and restrictions of human rights, are an accepted part of international human rights law. International human rights norms concerning derogations and restrictions can be found in a number of specific instruments including, The Siracusa Principles on the Limitation and Derogation Provisions in the International Covenant on Civil and Political Rights,[126] The Paris Minimum Standards of Human Rights Norms in a State of Emergency[127] and United Nations Human Rights Committee, General Comment No. 29: States of Emergency (article 4).[128] Notably, however, none of these standards consider economic, social and cultural rights, limiting their scope and content to questions concerning restrictions and derogations from civil and political

123 ibid 1.

124 Greene (n 8) 11.

125 ibid xiii.

126 International Commission of Jurists, Siracusa Principles on the Limitation and Derogation Provisions in the International Covenant on Civil and Political Rights (1985). https://www.icj.org/wp-content/uploads/1984/07/Siracusa-principles-ICCPR-legal-submission-1985-eng.pdf

127 International Law Association (ILA), The Paris Minimum Standards of Human Rights Norms in a State of Emergency (1984).

128 United Nations Human Rights Committee, General Comment No. 29: States of Emergency (Article 4), CCPR/C/21/Rev.1/Add.11 (31 August 2001).

rights.[129] Also significant is the recognition that to qualify as a legal 'state of emergency' a very high 'threat-severity threshold' must be met, that is, the emergency must be of a magnitude that 'threatens the life of the nation'.[130] Consequently, these requirements will only apply once this threshold has been crossed. As such, the question remains as to what restrictions can be placed upon the enjoyment of economic, social and cultural rights during such 'states of emergency' but also what limitations are permitted during crises that do not reach the threshold requirements of such emergency paradigms.

As set out in Chapter One, article 4 of the ICESCR provides the general limitations clause for the Covenant and determines the requirements for permissible limitations on the rights contained within the treaty. It is imperative to note that ICESCR does not contain any further clause permitting restrictions (save for the specific limitations set out in article 8). Nor does it contain any derogation clause. Alston and Quinn contend, there are three main reasons why this is the case:

> (1) the nature of the rights contained in the Covenant and the fact that the case for derogation in times of emergency from, for example, the rights to food or to health care would seem inherently less compelling than the case for derogation from the right of peaceful assembly or the

[129] It should be noted that the ILA has recently updated this work with a new report that considers emergencies including COVID-19 and the financial crisis. However, consideration of ESCRs is limited to noting the impacts of emergencies on such rights and the framework remains one of derogations and SOE. See ILA Final Report of the Committee on Human Rights in Times of Emergency, presented at the Athens Conference (2024), paras 18 f; 86; 14 and 15. https://www.ila-hq.org/en_GB/documents/ila-chrite-final-report-submitted-to-london-corrected-0824

[130] United Nations Human Rights Committee, General Comment No. 29: States of Emergency (Article 4), CCPR/C/21/Rev.1/Add.11 (31 August 2001) para. 3.

> right to vote; (2) the existence of a general limitations clause in the Covenant, unlike the approach adopted in the Covenant on Civil and Political Rights; and (3) the more flexible and accommodating nature of the basic obligation contained in article 2(1).[131]

Consequently, in most cases 'the requirement that limitations under the Covenant be compatible with the nature of the rights may, where appropriate, be interpreted as making some rights non-derogable'.[132] To derogate from basic survival rights would violate the minimum core – the very essence of the right in question and so would be incompatible with the nature of the right. Moreover, as Hartman notes, one of the two criteria for non-derogability of a right is that the 'right in question is essential to human dignity'.[133] This is also in line with Daes' basic principles governing limitations (as set out in Chapter One) whereby any limitation that does not respect and maintain the human dignity of the individual is unlawful.[134] As such, the minimum core of ESCRs must be non-derogable.[135]

---

[131] Alston and Quinn (n 82) 193.

[132] ibid 219.

[133] J.F. Hartman, 'Derogation from Human Rights Treaties in Public Emergencies', (1981) 22(1) *Harvard International Law Journal* 15.

[134] See Chapter One; Daes (n 20) 178, para. 1055.

[135] See UN Committee on Economic, Social and Cultural Rights, General Comment No. 14 (2000) The right to the highest attainable standard of health (article 12 of the International Covenant on Economic, Social and Cultural Rights), E/C.12/2000/4 (11 August 2000), para. 47, stressing that a State cannot justify non-compliance with its core obligations which are non-derogable; Committee on Economic, Social and Cultural Rights, General Comment No. 15 (2002) The right to water (articles 11 and 12 of the International Covenant on Economic, Social and Cultural Rights) E/C.12/2002/11 (20 January 2003), para. 40, reiterating that the core contents of the right are non-derogable); Committee On Economic, Social and Cultural Rights, Substantive Issues Arising in the Implementation of the International Covenant on Economic, Social and Cultural Rights: Poverty and the International Covenant on Economic,

Moreover, it is unnecessary to derogate from the wider scope of ESCRs as the scope can be progressively realised and if a State Party fails to 'take steps' the doctrine of non-retrogression under article 2(1) can be applied.[136] It is also argued that the general limitations clause 'would generally be sufficient to enable a state party to respond to an emergency situation in compliance with its obligations under the Covenant',[137] without the need to derogate from provisions. This combination of the article 4 general limitations clause plus the flexibility provided by article 2(1) general obligations clause and the central concept of progressive realisation, ensures that a derogations clause is unnecessary.[138]

Somewhat surprisingly, Alston and Quinn conclude that:

> Where the situation appears to be sufficiently grave as to warrant derogation the absence of a specific derogation clause from the Covenant should not be interpreted as foreclosing such a possibility; [...] where derogation is undertaken a state party should be required to satisfy the criteria applicable under the Covenant on Civil and Political Rights; (Siracusa Principles 7–9) and (4).[139]

However, this interpretation would seem to counter the intention of the drafters of the ICESCR who unambiguously did not include a derogation provision, clearly believing article 4 to suffice. As such, I would argue that derogations

Social and Cultural Rights, Statement Adopted by the Committee on Economic, Social and Cultural Rights, on the 4 May 2001, E/C.12/2001/10 (10 May 2001), paras 16–18, stating that the core contents of these rights are non-derogable.

136 See latter discussion on the overlap between article 2(1) and article 4.

137 Alston and Quinn (n 82) 219.

138 Manisuli Ssenyonjo, 'Reflections on State Obligations with Respect to Economic, Social and Cultural Rights in International Human Rights Law' (2010) 15(6) *The International Journal of Human Rights* 969, 991.

139 Alston and Quinn (n 82) 219.

of ESCRs under the Covenant are not permitted under any circumstances.[140]

2.2 Limitations of ESCRs in specific crises – what have we learnt to date?

2.2.1 Article 4 limitations of national security and public emergencies

Given the legal interpretation of article 4, it is interesting to note that previously, Alston and Quinn found that empirically governments most commonly sought to limit economic and social rights by reference to concerns for national security.[141] However, they argue that article 4 is unequivocal in its wording and 'such reasons can legitimately be invoked only in so far as they are genuinely synonymous with "the general welfare"' in society.[142]

Conversely, Giacca argues that 'article 4 needs to be read in light of other relevant rules of human rights law in the field of civil and political rights, precisely because objectives such as public order and national security are absent from article 4'.[143]

---

[140] Exceptionally, under the doctrine of *force majeure* a state can argue its non-compliance with its treaty obligations under the ICESCR due to 'the occurrence of an irresistible force or of an unforeseen event, beyond the control of the State, making it materially impossible in the circumstances to perform the obligation' (Article 23, International Law Commission (ILC) Draft Articles on the Responsibility of States for Internationally Wrongful Acts Art 23(1), 12 December 2001, A/Res/56/83). However, 'to date the CESCR has not acknowledged the possibility of derogating from the Covenant's obligations including the use of *force majeure*' (Sepúlveda (n 88) 303). See also Draft Articles on Responsibility of States for Internationally Wrongful Acts, with Commentaries 2001, 77, 78. https://legal.un.org/ilc/texts/instruments/english/commentaries/9_6_2001.pdf

[141] Alston and Quinn (n 82) 202.

[142] ibid.

[143] Giacca (n 3) 68.

Arguably though the absence of such explicit grounds within the text of the article indicates that the drafters never intended for ESCRs to be subject to limitations on such grounds. As noted previously, the *travaux préparatoires* evidence that it was intended that 'the purposes for which limitations may be imposed are arguably narrower than those specified in other human rights instruments'.[144]

Moreover, as noted previously, because there is no derogations clause within the ICESCR (as opposed to the derogations clause found in the ICCPR for example), this would bolster the argument that exemptions from human rights obligations on the grounds of national security, were not envisaged by the drafters as desirable or necessary under the Covenant.[145]

When examining the question of article 4 limitations on the grounds of national security, it is evident that on an international level there has been minimal engagement to formulate a policy or standard regarding emergencies and economic, social and cultural rights generally or specifically in relation to national security or public emergencies. However, as will be explored in Chapter Three, in line with Alston and Quinn's previous research, there is substantive empirical evidence of state practice in using such grounds to limit economic and social rights at a domestic level.

2.2.2 Article 4 limitations and the economic crisis – de facto limitations and the nexus with article 2(1)

The advent of the financial crisis in 2008 provided impetus for both States and human rights bodies (as well as scholars) to examine the application of article 4 ICESCR in times of

[144] Alston and Quinn (n 82) 193. See also Chapter One.

[145] See also Daes (n 20) 202, para. 163, arguing that 'no exceptions are provided for in cases of public emergency'.

crisis, in this case an economic crisis. While debate ensued as to whether such a crisis could constitute a legal state of emergency,[146] for the purposes of ICESCR the engagement of article 4 was unequivocal. What became increasingly evident was that the intersection between article 4 as the general limitation clause and article 2(1) the general obligations clause, in particular the fundamental concepts of progressive realisation and the prohibition of retrogressive measures, is crucial to the development of understanding permissible limitations on ESCRs in this context.

The financial crisis and the imposition of austerity measures in response resulted in severe negative impacts on the realisation of economic and social rights across a number of states.[147] This ensured that the UN CESCR when reviewing States Parties periodic reports under the ICESCR were increasingly faced with states who, due to a reduction of resources, were imposing cuts to social provision, for example, abolishing benefits or introducing benefit caps and introducing public sector pays freezes (which resulted in real term pay cuts).[148] Such measures resulted in stagnation or retrogression in the enjoyment of ESCRs and the Committee needed to respond to this crisis.

In 2012, the CESCR issued an Open Letter from the Chair on behalf of the CESCR[149] in an attempt to clarify

[146] Greene (n 8) 60.

[147] Amanda Cahill-Ripley and Luke David Graham, 'Using Community-Based Truth Commissions to Address Poverty and Related Economic, Social and Cultural Rights Violations: The UK Poverty Truth Commissions as Transformative Justice' (2021) *Journal of Human Rights Practice* 225–49.

[148] ibid 228.

[149] Chairperson of the CESCR, 'Letter Dated 16 May 2012 Addressed by the Chairperson of the Committee on Economic, Social and Cultural Rights to States Parties to the International Covenant on Economic, Social and Cultural Rights' (2012) UN Doc HRC/NONE/2012/76, UN reference CESCR/48th/SP/MAB/SW.

the position of States Parties regarding their legal obligations in such circumstances. The Letter stated, that while the Committee noted:

> the pressure on many States parties to embark on austerity programmes, sometimes severe, in the face of rising public deficits and poor economic growth [...] under the Covenant all States parties should avoid at all times taking decisions which might lead to the denial or infringement of economic, social and cultural rights.[150]

As Warwick notes, the statement that 'States should "avoid at all times" denials of socio-economic rights' is 'weak phrasing' and appears to dilute the legal obligation for States Parties who 'should not' violate socio-economic rights.[151] This is especially true given that 'endeavours to protect the most basic economic, social and cultural rights become more, rather than less, urgent' in times of crisis including times of austerity.[152] Further, in para. 6 the Letter set out what has been deemed a 'pseudo-derogation test'[153] whereby States who have to make 'inevitable adjustments' to the implementation of Covenant rights had to meet the following stated requirements:

> first, the policy is a *temporary* measure covering only the period of crisis; Second, the policy is *necessary* and *proportionate*, in the sense that the adoption of any other policy, or a failure to act, would be more detrimental to economic, social and cultural rights; Third, the

---

[150] ibid paras 2, 3.

[151] Ben T.C. Warwick, 'Socio-Economic Rights During Economic Crises: A Changed Approach to Non-Retrogression' (2016) 65 *International and Comparative Law Quarterly* 256.

[152] CESCR, 'General Comment 2: International Technical Assistance Measures' (1990) UN Doc E/1990/23, para. 9.

[153] Warwick (n 151) 261.

> policy is not discriminatory and must comprise all possible measures, including tax measures, to support social transfers to mitigate inequalities that can grow in times of crisis and to ensure that the rights of the disadvantaged and marginalized individuals and groups are not disproportionately affected; Fourth, the policy identifies the minimum core content of rights or a social protection floor, as developed by the International Labour Organization, and *ensures protection of this core content* at all times.[154]

While the requirements set out in the Letter clearly echoed broader principles around restrictions of human rights, using concepts of necessity, proportionality and temporality, the Committee did not refer to article 4 and did not encourage States Parties to utilise or engage with article 4 despite evidence of de facto limitations on Covenant rights. Instead, the CESCR focused predominantly on article 2(1) and the concept of retrogression. The argument for such an approach can be found in the doctrinal rationale that 'Article 4 was clearly seen by its drafters as dealing with limitations other than those that could be imposed under article 2(1) on the grounds of limited resource availability.'[155] However, the engagement of article 4 'is intimately related to the general obligations assumed by state parties in accordance with article 2(1) of the Covenant'.[156] The question raised is whether ESCRs during the economic crisis may have been better protected through viewing such retrogressive measures as de facto limitations,

[154] Chairperson of the CESCR (n 149) para. 7. Emphasis added.

[155] Alston and Quinn (n 82) 194; See also Giacca (n 3) 72; Müller (n 2) 570; Matthew Craven, *The International Covenant on Economic, Social and Cultural Rights: A Perspective on Its Development* (Clarendon Press, 1998) 132 and 214–15; Sepúlveda (n 88) 277–92.

[156] Alston and Quinn (n 82) 193.

which required formalisation, thus leading to greater scrutiny under the requirements of article 4.

Moreover, the introduction of the idea that retrogressive measures could now be justified was a move away from the previous rule that such measures were *prima facie* a violation of the Covenant.[157] A similar conception of retrogressive measures can be found in the CESCR, Statement on Public Debt in 2016 which provides:

> If the adoption of retrogressive measures is unavoidable, such measures should be *necessary* and *proportionate*, in the sense that the adoption of any other policy or failure to act would be more detrimental to economic, social and cultural rights. They should remain in place only insofar as they are necessary; they should not result in discrimination; they should mitigate inequalities that can grow in times of crisis and ensure that the rights of disadvantaged and marginalized individuals and groups are not disproportionately affected; and they should not affect the minimum core content of the rights protected under the Covenant.[158]

In this sense, retrogressive measures appear to be conceptualised as a form of limitations, engaging requirements of necessity, proportionality, temporality and review (and non-discrimination). Moreover, this new interpretation of non-retrogression Warwick argues has 'the potential to shift

[157] Judith Bueno de Mesquita, Claire Lougarre, Lisa Montel and Sharifah Sekalala, 'Lodestar in the Time of Coronavirus? Interpreting International Obligations to Realise the Right to Health During the COVID-19 Pandemic' (2023) 23 *Human Rights Law Review* 1, 19.

[158] Committee on Economic, Social and Cultural Rights, 'Statement Public Debt, Austerity Measures and the International Covenant on Economic, Social and Cultural Rights' UN Doc E/C.12/2016/1 (22 July 2016), para. 4. Emphasis added.

substantially the interpretation of the doctrine [...] and perhaps consequently of the Covenant—by moving towards a model of emergency "accommodation"'.[159] In other words, the response of the Committee appeared to endorse an 'emergency paradigm' for Covenant rights, setting out how such rights should be interpreted in a 'state of emergency'. Moreover, the so called 'pseudo-derogation test' arguably appears to reduce state obligations in such a crisis even further by providing an additional 'flexibility' mechanism in addition to the existing flexibility provided by article 4 alongside article 2(1).[160]

In sum, it is clear that the previous strict enforcement model that applied to non-retrogression was challenged by the advent of the 2008 economic crisis and the Committee's response to the resulting austerity measures. By changing their approach from one which operated under a 'business as usual' model of the ICESCR,[161] to an 'emergency exceptional approach',[162] the interpretation of both article 4 and article 2(1) has been called into question. Crucially, it may also have deterred States Parties from actually invoking article 4 limitations as they could avoid the scrutiny of permissible limitations and justify de facto limitations instead under article 2(1).

2.2.3 Article 4 limitations and public health crises – balancing rights

Most recently, the impact of the global COVID-19 pandemic has again ensured international human rights bodies have had to consider the implications of a global emergency upon the enjoyment of ESCRs. During the pandemic, the focus of permissible limitations had been on balancing rights

159 Warwick (n 151) 255.
160 ibid 263.
161 ibid 253.
162 ibid.

with public health concerns. In their 2020 Statement on the Coronavirus Disease (COVID-19) Pandemic and Economic, Social and Cultural Rights, the Committee noted that any measures taken to limit economic, social and cultural rights because of the pandemic, 'should comply with the conditions set out in article 4 of the Covenant'; must be 'necessary to combat the public health crisis posed by COVID 19'; and be 'reasonable and proportionate'.[163] In this context the explicit application of article 4 rather than use of article 2(1) is clear.

However, rather than reiterating the triple requirements of article 4, the requirements of reasonableness and proportionality are prioritised. Such requirements are a relatively new development by the Committee as will be discussed in the empirical analysis section later.[164] For now, it is sufficient to point out that the Statement provides a strong move towards an emergency model, as mentioned previously, by explicitly drawing upon standards set out in the Siracusa Principles on the Limitation and Derogation Provisions in the International Covenant on Civil and Political Rights (1984)[165] (designed for civil and political rights). As Bueno de Mesquita et al argue:

> These Principles have become an influential framework to navigate the protection of human rights in emergencies including public health emergencies such as COVID-19. Though developed with civil and political rights in mind, General Comment 14 suggests their relevance to interpreting permissible limitations to economic, social and cultural rights under the ICESCR's limitations clause (article 4) [...].[166]

[163] Committee on Economic, Social and Cultural Rights, 'Statement on the Coronavirus Disease (COVID-19) Pandemic and Economic, Social and Cultural Rights', E/C.12/2020/1 (17 April 2020), para. 11.

[164] See Chapter Three.

[165] International Commission of Jurists, Siracusa Principles (n 126).

[166] Bueno de Mesquita et al (n 157), 14.

In fact, General Comment 14, clearly and explicitly draws upon the limitations regime for the ICCPR, setting out specific grounds for permissible limitations,

> a State party which, for example, restricts the movement of, or incarcerates, persons with transmissible diseases [...] on grounds such as *national security* or the *preservation of public order*, has the burden of justifying such serious measures in relation to each of the elements identified in article 4. Such restrictions must be in accordance with the law, including international human rights standards, compatible with the nature of the rights protected by the Covenant, in the interest of legitimate aims pursued, and strictly necessary for the promotion of the general welfare in a democratic society.[167]

In addition, they state that:

> such limitations must be *proportional*, i.e. the least restrictive alternative must be adopted where several types of limitations are available. Even where such limitations on grounds of protecting public health are basically permitted, they should be of limited duration and subject to review.[168]

Further evidence of an emergency accommodation model can be seen in the omission of an unequivocal statement by the Committee on the absolute nature of minimum core obligations or protecting the essential minimum core content during the crisis. In para. 12 of the 2020 Statement on the Coronavirus Disease (COVID-19), the CESCR state that the 'minimum core obligations imposed by the Covenant should be

[167] UN CESCR General Comment No. 14 (n 135) para. 28. Emphasis added.
[168] ibid para. 29. Emphasis added.

prioritized'.[169] They then footnote General Comment No. 3, para. 10 which provides that states can validate a failure to meet such core obligations if 'every effort has been made to use all resources that are at its disposition in an effort to satisfy, as a matter of priority, those minimum obligations'.[170] Compare this with the inviolability of the minimum core, even in times of emergency as set out in the Office of the High Commissioner for Human Rights (OHCHR) on Emergency Measures and COVID-19 which clearly states, 'State obligations associated with the *core content* of the rights to food, health, housing, social protection, water and sanitation, education and an adequate standard of living remain in effect even during situations of emergency'[171] as well as being previously asserted in a number of General Comments, including General Comment 14 on Health.[172] Moreover, the guidance continues, that even

[169] Committee on Economic, Social and Cultural Rights, (n 163) para. 12. Emphasis added.

[170] CESCR, 'General Comment No. 3: The Nature of States Parties' Obligations (Art. 2, Para. 1 of the Covenant)' E/1991/23 (14 December 1990), para. 10. Other examples see General Comment No. 25 (2020) on science and economic, social and cultural rights (articles 15 (1) (b), (2), (3) and (4) of the International Covenant on Economic, Social and Cultural Rights) para. 51; General Comment No. 19 The right to social security (article 9) E/C.12/GC/19 (4 February 2008), para. 60. Cf with General Comment No. 15 (2002) The right to water (articles 11 and 12 of the International Covenant on Economic, Social and Cultural Rights), E/C.12/2002/11 (20 January 2003), para. 40; UN CESCR General Comment No. 14 (n 135) para. 47.

[171] OHCHR Emergency Measures and COVID-19:
Topics in Focus, Guidance (27 April 2020), p 1 para. 5. Emphasis added. https://www.ohchr.org/sites/default/files/Documents/Events/EmergencyMeasures_COVID19.pdf

[172] UN CESCR General Comment No. 14 (n 135) para. 47. Also, Committee on Economic, Social and Cultural Rights, 'Statement Public Debt, Austerity Measures and the International Covenant on Economic,

if a legal state of emergency is declared and derogations or restrictions are placed upon civil and political rights:

> States should provide timely and effective measures to support the enjoyment of core economic and social rights of people affected by emergency restrictions, including through support for employment and livelihoods, housing, food, education, social protection and health, in order to enable them to comply with the emergency measures.[173]

Thus as Bueno de Mesquita et al highlight, 'The CESCR, nonetheless, keeps sending confusing messages regarding the absolute nature of such obligations, that is, the possibility to restrict them at any given time.'[174] Fundamentally, 'by failing to recognise the absolute/non-derogable (and thus, immediate) nature of core obligations in times of COVID-19, [...] the CESCR has declined to set universal standards applying to all States' and missed an opportunity to ensure they could hold states to account 'in future global health emergencies'.[175] In sum, the absolute nature of the minimum core obligations, even during emergencies, has been undermined by the response to the pandemic and the economic crisis as noted previously.

In addition, the confusion over whether retrogression could be permitted under exceptional circumstances that was seen in the economic crisis was similarly as issue in the response to COVID-19. 'In General Comments 3 and 14, the CESCR declares that States' obligation to progressively

Social and Cultural Rights', UN Doc E/C.12/2016/1 (22 July 2016), para. 4.

173 OHCHR Emergency Measures and COVID-19: Guidance, 27 April 2020, at p 3.

174 Bueno de Mesquita et al (n 157) 22.

175 ibid 21.

realise the right to health presumes an impermissibility of retrogressive measures.'[176] Yet as Bueno de Mesquita et al note, the CESCR:

> also declares that retrogressive measures are allowed if States can prove they carefully considered all alternatives and can justify such measures by reference to all the other rights protected in the ICESCR, in light of their maximum available resources. However, the COVID-19 context renders the interpretation of non-retrogression difficult, given some measures to progressively prevent, treat and control COVID-19 entailed in practice retrogressive measures for other right to health entitlements, for example, pausing cancer screening or interruptions to sexual and reproductive healthcare.[177]

Accordingly, this issue, which primarily centres on balancing one aspect of the right to health against another, could have perhaps been better managed through applying the requirements of article 4 and assessing what limitations were lawful, compatible with the nature of the right to health and for the general welfare of society.

Moreover, as discussed previously, rather than utilise article 4 of the Covenant, the CESCR considered restrictions on the right to health due to COVID-19 through the lens of the Siracusa Principles, noting that ' that public health measures should be proportionate, necessary and in accordance with the law'.[178] Although these principles have been referred to

---

[176] ibid 19. See, for example, CESCR, 'General Comment No. 3: The Nature of States Parties' Obligations (Art. 2, Para. 1 of the Covenant)', UN Doc E/1991/23 (14 December 1990), para. 9; UN CESCR General Comment No. 14 (n 135) para. 32.

[177] ibid.

[178] Committee on Economic, Social and Cultural Rights, (n 163) para. 3.

previously in the context of interpreting the right to health,[179] it remains unclear as to why the Committee did not consider the limitations clause that is provided for under the ICESCR.

In sum, while the pandemic presented different challenges to the economic crisis, it also illustrated the common tensions around article 4 limitations and the Committee's willingness to put in place an emergency or accommodation regime for interpreting ESCRs, rather than adopting a 'business as usual' strict interpretation of the legal framework provided for under article 4 ICESCR. This may be due to leanings towards incorporating elements of the emergency regime for civil and political rights, the confusion around the interpretation of article 4 together with article 2(1) and the tension as to whether minimum core content can be restricted. In its response to the COVID-19 crisis, 'the CESCR did not provide a clear answer to these normative and practical questions'.[180] In response to the lack of sufficient, clear guidance in 2023, The Global Health Law Consortium and the International Commission of Jurists drafted 'The Principles and Guidelines on Human Rights and Public Health Emergencies'.[181] Consisting of five sections with 28 paragraphs in total, the issue of limitations is dealt with in para. 16. Unfortunately, the provision refers only to the requirements of the Siracusa Principles, such that States must have 'strict regard for the principles of legality, necessity, proportionality and non-discrimination'.[182] The

[179] See UN CESCR General Comment No. 14 (n 135) para. 28.

[180] Roman Girma Teshome, 'Derogations to Human Rights During a Global Pandemic: Unpacking Normative and Practical Challenges' (2022) 37(2) *American University International Law Review* 307–54 at 346.

[181] 'The Principles and Guidelines on Human Rights and Public Health Emergencies' 10 May 2023, (2024) 1(1) *Journal of Global Health Law* 122–43 (also at www.PHEPrinciples.org).

[182] ibid para. 16.1.

Principles do not refer to article 4 ICESCR requirements whatsoever.[183]

In conclusion, it is evident that the pandemic has provided another context in which the question of limitations on economic, social and cultural rights has been emphasised. As Forman and Kohler contend, the experience of 'COVID-19 thus underscores the urgent need for clearer rules about legitimate restrictions of the right to health,'[184] and I would argue all ESCRs.

2.2.4 Article 4 limitations and conflict-affected settings

Finally, the question of permissible limitations in the context of a conflict-affected setting (CAS), has not been specifically considered by the Committee or indeed by scholars.[185] However, in the contemporary global context of increasing armed conflicts and threats to global security such as climate change, the extent of the restrictions states are permitted to put on the enjoyment of ESCRs is pertinent. The question of the applicability of the ICESCR in times of armed conflict has been settled,[186] and international humanitarian law guides

[183] Similarly, the Principles refer to retrogression in para. 12 but rather than clarify the inviolability of minimum core obligations, they reinforce the justification of retrogressive measures.

[184] Lisa Forman and Jillian Clare Kohler, 'Global Health and Human Rights in the Time of COVID-19: Response, Restrictions and Legitimacy' (2020) 19 *Journal of Human Rights* 547, 547.

[185] For the purposes of this book, the term 'conflict' refers to armed conflict. The term 'conflict affected settings', refers to any setting in that has been affected by armed conflict, although the current situation may not meet the threshold to be deemed an international armed conflict or a non-international armed conflict as determined under international humanitarian law. CAS is a useful term intended to capture war, transitional and post-conflict situations.

[186] See Legal Consequences of the Construction of a Wall in the Occupied Palestinian Territory, Advisory Opinion, I. C. J. Reports 2004, p 136 (9 July 2004), para. 106; see, for example, inter alia, CESCR, Concluding

the applicability of the ICESCR during armed conflict acting as the *lex specialis*.[187] In addition, the minimum core principle, guides the application of ICESCR ensuring that the minimum core of ESCRs cannot be derogated from during armed conflict.[188] As Riedel argues, 'on no account can the rights to health, to food, housing, access to water, or to education be set aside in respect of their core content, even during times of armed conflict'.[189]

As regards limitations, as noted above the situation is less clear. In addition, the extent of states' obligations under ICESCR in transitional or post-conflict situations (as opposed to a situation classified as international or non-international armed conflict under international humanitarian law) has received little attention. Based upon Daes' basic principles for restrictions and the requirements of article 4 itself:

> in principle even in times of armed conflict or general emergency the Covenant rights have to be upheld, as

observations on the fourth periodic report of Israel, E/C.12/ISR/CO/4 (12 November 2019), para. 9; CESCR Concluding Observations concerning the initial report of the Central African Republic, E/C.12/CAF/CO/1 (4 May 2018); Amanda Cahill-Ripley, *The Human Right to Water and Its Application in the Occupied Palestinian Territories* (Routledge 2011) 84–5.

187 The debate over *lex specialis* in times of occupation or protracted conflict is less clear. See Cahill-Ripley (n 186), 135; Noam Lubell, 'Challenges in Applying Human Rights Law to Armed Conflict' (2005) 87(860) *International Review of the Red Cross* 737–54.

188 UN Committee on Economic, Social and Cultural Rights, Substantive Issues Arising in the Implementation of the International Covenant on Economic, Social and Cultural Rights: Poverty and the International Covenant on Economic, Social and Cultural Rights, Statement Adopted by the Committee on Economic, Social and Cultural Rights, on 4 May 2001, E/C.12/2001/10 (10 May 2001), para. 18.

189 Eibe Riedel, 'Economic, Social, and Cultural Rights in Armed Conflict' in Andrew Clapham and Paola Gaeta (eds), *The Oxford Handbook of International Law in Armed Conflict* (OUP 2014) 441–68, 463.

> far as their core content is concerned. In fact, in [those] crisis situations, the population generally, but in particular marginalized and disadvantaged individuals and groups within society, are in even greater need of protection than in peacetime. Thus, while the ICCPR expressly names specific rights, which can be limited in times of conflict, albeit with limitations, the ICESCR has broader application, and assumes that in principle each Covenant right maintains its validity, even in times of an emergency.[190]

It is imperative to remember however, that situations of armed conflict (or transitional contexts) are not automatically legal 'states of emergency' (SOE). In relation to civil and political rights this is explicitly recognised:

> Not every disturbance or catastrophe qualifies as a public emergency which threatens the life of the nation, as required by article 4, paragraph 1. During armed conflict, whether international or non-international, rules of international humanitarian law become applicable and help, in addition to the provisions in article 4 and article 5, paragraph 1, of the Covenant, to prevent the abuse of a State's emergency powers. The Covenant requires that even during an armed conflict measures derogating from the Covenant are allowed only if and to the extent that the situation constitutes a threat to the life of the nation.[191]

Furthermore, as determined previously, if a SOE is deemed to exist by the state, then article 4 still applies as in peacetime

---

[190] ibid.

[191] CCPR, General Comment No. 29 States of Emergency (Article 4) CCPR/C/21/Rev.1/Add.11 (31 August 2001), para. 3. Cf this with State perceptions however, where war is frequently equated with a State of Emergency in their constitutional law. See Greene (n 8) 15.

(normality). The application of socio-economic rights in such a conflict-affected settings thus supports the argument that equating limitations on ESCRs with the framework for CPRs, that is, based upon emergency regimes and derogations is not helpful. Due to the very difference in their nature, the application of ESCRs in crisis of any kind should not be conflated with the application of CPRs in states of emergency.

Moreover, importantly in situations of transition and post-conflict or protracted conflict, the normal ESCRs legal framework applies.[192] Protracted conflicts by their very nature exist for a long period and a 'crisis orientation'[193] for international human rights law in such a context, does not deal adequately with the situation on the ground, which can intermittently reflect conditions of peacetime more than war, and crucially can require tackling structural violence and a lack of development. Such a position will also avoid what Greene has called a 'legal black hole' that is, becoming lost in a perpetual crisis state.[194]

The practice of the CESCR concerning article 4 and conflict-affected settings is severely limited.[195] Within the 26 General Comments of the Committee, nine refer to the impacts of armed conflict upon the application of the Covenant in some

192 Although it may be complemented by various additional frameworks such as transitional justice and peacebuilding measures. See Amanda Cahill-Ripley, *Economic, Social and Cultural Rights and Peacebuilding* (forthcoming Cambridge University Press, 2026).

193 Hilary Charlesworth, 'International Law: A Discipline of Crisis' (2002) 65(3) *The Modern Law Review* 377–92, 386.

194 Greene (n 8) 99–146.

195 A total of 80 recommendations can be found over 37 documents that include reference to armed conflict within the work of the CESCR. For a full analysis of over 400 documents of the CESCRs' work concerning the Covenant and armed conflict including General Comments, Statements, Annual Reports (29) and Concluding Observations see Cahill-Ripley (n 192).

way.[196] However, there is only one instance where article 4 and conflict are considered relationally, CESCR General Comment 7 on Housing and Forced Evictions (1997) para. 5. This provides that any forced evictions that take place in conflict-affected settings must comply with the triple test under article 4.[197] Moreover, generally, the CESCR have issued recommendations for conflict-affected states in a number of Concluding Observations, but none of these has concerned the interaction between article 4 limitations and the enjoyment of ESCRs in conflict-affected settings. Rather, the impact of armed conflict upon the general enjoyment of ESCRs within States Parties is most often recognised as 'C'. Factors and difficulties impeding the implementation of the Covenant'[198]or 'Principal Subjects of Concern and Recommendations'[199] or 'Application of the Covenant in the Context of Armed Conflict'.[200] In addition, analysis of the jurisprudence of the CESCR reveals no communications to

196 UN CESCR General Comments, No. 7 (1997); No. 12 (1999) E/C.12/1999/5; No. 14 (2000) E/C.12/2000/4; 15 (2002) E/C.12/2002/11; No. 19 (2007) E/C.12/GC/19; No. 21 (2009) E/C.12/GC/21; No. 22 (2016) E/C.12/GC/22; No. 23 (2016) E/C.12/GC/23; No. 26 (2022) E/C.12/GC/26.

197 UN CESCR General Comment No. 7: The right to adequate housing (article 11 (1) of the Covenant): Forced evictions (16 May 1997), para. 5. See also paras 6 and 7.

198 For example, Concluding Observations Iraq E/C.12/1/Add.17 (12 December 1997), C. Factors and difficulties impeding the implementation of the Covenant, para. 7.

199 For example, Committee on Economic, Social and Cultural Rights Concluding observations on the sixth periodic report of the Democratic Republic of the Congo, E/C.12/COD/CO/6 (28 March 2022), C. Principal subjects of concern and recommendations, para. 4.

200 For example, Concluding observations on the third periodic report of Yemen E/C.12/YEM/CO/3 (23 March 2023), C. Principal subjects of concern and recommendations, Application of the Covenant in the context of armed conflict, para. 4.

date that have specifically concerned article 4 limitations and conflict affected settings or, natural disasters.[201]

What is significant, and can act as a building block for inclusion of article 4 consideration in such contexts, is the recognition by the CESCR of the restrictions upon the states' abilities to implement fully the rights under the Covenant due to a lack of effective control over some or all of its territory.[202] In CAS more than other types of crisis, de facto limitations upon the enjoyment of ESCRs are often beyond the control of the State Party, being a consequence of direct harms from the 'warring party' or indirect harms due to ongoing impacts of conflict. The Committee note that in such situations the State remains the primary obligation holder with a duty to 'endeavour, as far as possible, to fulfil its obligations under the Covenant by resorting to all means compatible with international law'.[203] In such instances, the Committee could insist that any obligations to realise the wider scope and substance of ESCRs, over and above the minimum core could be subject to article 4 limitations if the state was unable to comply with them. In conjunction with clarifying the minimum core in such conflict-affected settings[204] and with an emphasis on scrutinising the states' effort utilising the related principles of maximum available resources

[201] A search of OHCHR Jurisprudence Database http://juris.ohchr.org (9 April 2021) revealed no results on article 4 or conflict. An updated search of the database on 10 July 2022 found no results on a search of 'article 4 and conflict' or 'armed conflict'.

[202] CESCR (n 200) para. 5.

[203] ibid.

[204] As of March 2025, the CESCR is due to embark on a programme of work to draft a new General Comment on the application of the ICESCR in situations of armed conflict. This will include consideration of the scope and substance of minimum core obligations in times of armed conflict. Cahill-Ripley argues for a basic needs model for ESCRs during armed conflict utilising International humanitarian law as a starting point (survival rights) plus elements pertaining to human dignity and equality. See Cahill-Ripley (n 186) 44; Cahill-Ripley (n 192).

including international assistance, article 4 could be a useful tool for ensuring states comply with their full obligations under the Covenant in such difficult contexts, while ensuring ongoing scrutiny.

Another important factor to consider is that in practice, many ESCRs limitations in such situations are de facto limitations due to resource scarcity or lack of accessibility to existing resources, the latter of which could also relate to personal security issues. These de facto limitations could be short-term due to physical obstacles, or due to the destruction of resources, or could be a consequence of longer-term resource issues, as seen in protracted conflicts. For example, a lack of enjoyment of the right to water could be a result of direct damage to the water infrastructure through armed conflict. However, it could also be due to limited water supply due to the impacts of a protracted conflict such as displacement, lack of electricity or reduced economic access. Such actions whether deliberate or not, result in water scarcity and resource limitations. People have de facto restricted access to water.

The resulting situations could be determined as a breach of article 2(1) by the state in question (the de facto restrictions resulting in retrogression) or it could be justified through the rationale of General Comment 3, para. 10, that is, 'justified by reference to the totality of the rights provided for in the Covenant and in the context of the full use of the maximum available resources'[205] (characterised as non-compliance rather than a violation). Alternatively, though they could be dealt with under article 4, with the wider scope of the right to water being justifiably limited to ensure everyone has the minimal essential level of water. Obviously, if the state prevented access to any water or discriminated in supply of water, this would be impermissible and a violation of their obligations. The benefit of invoking article 4 would be to ensure transparency of state actions or omissions, increased scrutiny of the impacts of the restrictions and temporality of the limitations.

---

[205] CESCR General Comment No. 3 (n 170) para. 9.

The additional point here is that in such contexts it may be impossible to separate resource questions from security questions.[206] This brings us back to the question of the overlap and nexus between article 2(1) and article 4. Perhaps then, the practical experience of the enjoyment of ESCRs in conflict affected contexts leads us to the idea that article 2(1) and article 4 should be considered concurrently (as per CESCR General Comment 26 on Land).[207] However given the experience of the economic crisis and the public health crisis, it would seem that justifying de facto restrictions on the enjoyment of ESCRs utilising article 2(1) provides states with a wider discretion than if they invoke article 4.[208] As Alston and Quinn note, it would also 'allow states to justify limitations on a *de facto* basis under article 2(1) rather than on a *de jure* basis under article 4'.[209]

Alternatively, one might argue that permissible restrictions in such contexts should only apply article 4 in states of exception/emergency and that article 2(1) should be reserved for 'states of normality' or 'peacetime' only. However, as illustrated by the experience of the economic crisis and the COVID-19 pandemic, at times it may be necessary to limit ESCRs on the basis of resources and at other times due to the need to balance individual rights with the greater good of society. Moreover, as argued previously, article 4 does not operate as an emergency clause and does not trigger an emergency legal regime. Consequently, this latter model does not work either.

Müller argues for the merging of article 2(1) and article 4, stating that:

> it is unreasonable to make a distinction between, […], retrogressive measures in the progressive realisation of

[206] See also Müller (n 2) 590.

[207] See discussion in Chapter Three.

[208] Müller (n 2) 587.

[209] Alston and Quinn (n 82) 206.

> ESC rights because of resource constraints evaluated with reference to Article 2(1) ICESCR; and, […], limitations of ESC rights for other reasons, evaluating them against the criteria of Article 4.[210]

Consequently, she contends that 'a unified standard should be applied for evaluating all limitations, including retrogressive measures – namely the criteria just set out as required under Article 4'.[211] However, there is a clear distinction to me made between such concepts: *Intention*. 'Article 4 allows states to respond flexibly to situations of tension within a (democratic) society, including to situations of emergencies, without forcing them to breach their obligations under the ICESCR.'[212] Limitations put the onus on the state to think about what they can and cannot realise in that particular context. They then have to *actively restrict* the rights, according to the criteria set out in article 4. Conversely, although states are required to justify their lack of progression under article 2(1), retrogressive measures or stasis is passive – it means states can just claim they have tried to comply with their obligations while in reality allowing limits to ESCRs enjoyment. Consequently, it is argued that article 2(1) and article 4 should be kept as separate concepts with their specific purposes, as intended and set out in the *travaux préparatoires* to the ICESCR.[213]

Advocates of ESCRs have long argued for the application of the ICESCR during times of armed conflict. Consequently, the last thing that should be done now is to limit their application unnecessarily. In this way, there is a need to embrace an 'international law of everyday life'[214] meaning

[210] Müller (n 2) 585.

[211] ibid.

[212] ibid 600.

[213] Alston and Quinn (n 82) 205.

[214] Charlesworth (n 193) 377.

that in conflict-affected settings whether it be high intensity armed conflict, post-conflict (post-agreement) or transitional contexts, or indeed a situation of occupation or protracted conflict, no 'exceptional human rights legal regime' should apply. The existing legal framework for ESCRs can and arguably does apply in both CAS as in peacetime. Thus, ESCRs should be realised to the *maximum extent* possible in every situation. Minimum core should apply at all times, plus then whatever is possible given the particular situation. This can be assessed using the existing legal framework utilising the concept of progressive realisation provided in article 2(1) and the application of article 4 limitations as required.[215]

In sum, the existing legal framework of the Covenant can be applied in conflict affected settings more effectively by encouraging states to use article 4 limitations – is one tool that already exists to assist in the application of the ICESCR in such difficult times. When applied alongside clear minimum core obligations, utilising article 4 to realistically and temporarily limit the wider scope and content of ESCRs ensures legality, transparency, monitoring and review, while reassuring States Parties that their efforts to implement the Covenant where possible are recognised. It also ensures that States Parties cannot shirk their obligations or limit such rights unnecessarily and without scrutiny.

2.3 Concluding remarks

In conclusion, it is clear that the ICESCR does not provide for an emergency regime and that article 4 is not an emergency clause. Consequently, whether a situation can be deemed a legal 'state of emergency' or a 'crisis' (that is, not meeting the

[215] See Cahill-Ripley (n 192), for a detailed overview of obligations concerning ESCRs during such situations.

threshold of a legal state of emergency) or indeed whether classified as a situation of normality, article 4 applies. There is no requirement of an emergency to engage article 4. It is also important to highlight that as a consequence, no derogations are permitted from ICESCR, even in times of a state of emergency or crisis.

The advantage of such a constant and broad applicability of article 4 is that it can be applied across all situations regardless – in liminal contexts such as transitional periods between war and peace or post-disaster when clarity over other legal regimes applicable is sometimes lacking. As Müller notes, 'There is no doubt that it is unrealistic to expect states to implement all aspects of every economic, social and cultural right in times of crisis to the same extent as in normal times.'[216] However, the use of the article 4 limitations clause (alongside the requirement of minimum core) would seem to be a logical way in which states can abide by their obligations under the Covenant whilst reflecting on the realities of difficult contexts.

Having reviewed several types of crises, it is evident that there are a number of differences in the approach taken to dealing with each specific crisis. However, there are also a number of commonalities identified: regardless of the crisis in question, article 4 ICESCR has not been used by the CESCR to interpret the permissible restrictions possible on ESCRs.

As regards the economic financial crisis, the focus was predominantly on non-retrogression and retrogressive measures under article 2(1). Clearly, the nature of the crisis lends itself to as assessment of resource questions (that are ultimately raised in all types of crises), and the application of article 2(1) provides flexibility through the concepts of progressive realisation, non-retrogression and maximum available resources. However, applying article 4 could have been beneficial as a way to

---

[216] Müller (n 2) 598.

ensure transparency and accountability of states, as well as the temporality of any measures taken restricting ESCRs due to austerity measures taken.

In the case of the health crisis caused by the COVID-19 pandemic, questions around permissible restrictions on ESCRs have been dealt with by referral to emergency regimes and standards on derogations and restrictions pertaining to civil and political rights. While this may be due to the more developed legal standards around states of emergency and civil and political rights (and their historical dominance in state constitutions as well as in international human rights law), in doing so the Committee have tended towards establishing practice, which erodes the non-derogable status of ESCRs, and hints at the development of an emergency paradigm for interpreting such rights in times of crisis.

In times of armed conflict, the question of article 4 permissible restrictions has not been dealt with at all. However, during all three crises examined, the Committee have encouraged states to consider any de facto limitations on rights enjoyment through the application of article 2(1) and justifications for any retrogression. However, the previous analysis has illustrated that the nature of the relationship between article 4 and article 2(1) is unclear. For example, 'it is not difficult to foresee situations in which states, rather than invoking article 4, would simply rely on the notion of progressive realization (to the maximum of their available resources) to justify any limitations on a *de facto* rather than a *de jure* basis'.[217] This conceptual confusion around the employment of article 4 and article 2(1) has the potential to affect state practice as will be examined empirically below.

Overall, the reasoning behind the approaches taken to date are unclear. It would seem likely though that the lack of legal development and interpretation of article 4 itself has prevented

[217] Alston and Quinn (n 82) 205.

a systematic and consistent approach to dealing with ESCRs in such crises. It is crucial therefore, to 'dig deeper', to examine the Committee's practice regarding limitations throughout their mandate but also to gain an insight into the use of article 4 by States Parties to the Covenant.

THREE

The International Covenant on Economic, Social and Cultural Rights 1966, Article 4: An Empirical Analysis

From the doctrinal analysis undertaken previously and the examination of the previous responses to the impact of crises on economic and social rights, it is clear that article 4 has been under examined and theorised. Consequently, the scope of article 4 and its subsequent interpretation remain unclear. Similarly, the application of article 4 limitations in practice has received minimal attention (with the exception of the COVID-19 pandemic and financial crisis as noted previously). Thus, it is important to analyse the application of article 4 in practice.[218] Accordingly, a deep dive analysis of practice was undertaken which examined the application and interpretation

[218] Empirical legal research is focused on law 'in action' and 'involves the systematic collection of information ("data") and its analysis according to some generally accepted method. Of central importance is the systematic nature of the process, both of collecting and analysing the information' (Frans Leeuw and Hans Schmeets, *Empirical Legal Research: A Guidance Book for Lawyers, Legislators and Regulators* (Edward Elgar Publishing, 2016) 4). See also, P. Ishwara Bhat, 'Empirical Legal Research: Nature, Features, and Expanding Horizons' in *Idea and Methods of Legal Research* (OUP 2019) 303–325; John Baldwin and Gwynn Davis, 'Empirical Research in Law' in Mark Tushnet, and Peter Cane (eds), *The Oxford Handbook of Legal Studies* (OUP 2005) 880–900.

of article 4 by the CESCR through its General Comments and Substantive Statements, Concluding Observations and jurisprudence under the Optional Protocol to the Covenant. This analysis focused on their use of article 4, generally, and in relation to the specific idea of crisis. Further, State Parties practice in terms of their periodic reports to the CESCR were also analysed. Finally, the question of limitations on ESCRs was examined under the UN Charter mechanisms: the Universal Periodic Review (UPR) and Special Procedures of the Human Rights Council. The findings are summarised and scrutinised later.

3.1 The approach of the CESCR – mapping interpretation and application of article 4 to date

Previously the practice of the CESCR has provided 'little interpretation of the legal parameters of the limitation provision or possible derogations from ESC rights'.[219] With this in mind, quantitative analysis and qualitative textual analysis of the practice of the CESCR was undertaken, with a view to further elucidating the parameters of permissible limitations as interpreted by the Committee.[220]

3.1.1 General Comments (and Substantive Statements)

Analysis was undertaken of the 26 General Comments that have been adopted by the CESCR to date.[221] Seven General

[219] Giacca (n 3) 72.

[220] Dataset on file with author. The data sample consisted of 443 documents up to and including the CESCR 71st session in March 2022; General Comments (26), Statements (19), Annual Reports (29) and Concluding Observations (369). The dataset was analysed using Atlas Ti 9. Ten codes were used including *inter alia* 'article 4'; 'limitations'. Additionally, Draft General Comment 26 was analysed.

[221] Analysis undertaken 29 March 2021 and again 10 July 2022.

Comments provided for article 4 limitations, spanning a period 1997–2022.[222] Over this period, it is evident that the Committee start to develop a more expansive interpretation of article 4: in General Comment 7 in 1997 we see the first provision relating specifically to article 4 within a General Comment where para. 5 sets out the original 'Triple Test' noting that 'any limitations imposed must be determined by law only insofar as this may be compatible with the nature of these rights and solely for the purpose of promoting the general welfare in a democratic society'.[223]

In the 1999 General Comment on the right to education, the Committee emphasised the nature of the limitations clause as 'primarily intended to be protective of the rights of individuals rather than permissive of the imposition of limitations by the State'.[224] However, they also raise the issue of limitations due to

[222] UN CESCR General Comment No. 7 (n 197); UN CESCR General Comment No. 13 (Twenty-first session, 1999) The right to education (article 13 of the Covenant) E/C.12/1999/10 (8 December 1999); UN CESCR General Comment No. 14 (n 135); UN CESCR General Comment No. 17 (2005) The right of everyone to benefit from the protection of the moral and material interests resulting from any scientific, literary or artistic production of which he or she is the author (article 15, paragraph 1 (c), of the Covenant) E/C.12/GC/17 (12 January 2006); UN CESCR General Comment No. 21 Right of everyone to take part in cultural life (article 15, para. 1 (a), of the International Covenant on Economic, Social and Cultural Rights) E/C.12/GC/21 (21 December 2009); UN CESCR General Comment No. 25 (2020) on science and economic, social and cultural rights (article 15 (1) (b), (2), (3) and (4) of the International Covenant on Economic, Social and Cultural Rights) E/C.12/GC/25 and E/C.12/GC/26 (30 April 2020); UN CESCR General Comment No. 26 (2022) on Land and Economic, Social and Cultural Rights and Draft General Comment No. 26 (2021) on land and economic, social and cultural rights (Draft prepared by the Rapporteurs, Rodrigo Uprimny and Michael Windfuhr, 3 May 2021, E/C.12/69/R.2).

[223] UN CESCR General Comment No. 7 (n 197) para. 5.

[224] UN CESCR General Comment No. 13 (n 222) Limitations on article 13, para. 42.

'national security' or 'the preservation of public order', neither of which are explicitly provided for as legitimate reasons for restricting ESCRs under article 4. They note that any state which imposes limitations on these grounds 'has the burden of justifying such a serious measure in relation to each of the elements identified in article 4'.[225] The inclusion of such grounds seemingly expands the legitimate reasons for limiting ESCRs and draws upon the requirements for derogations or restrictions under civil and political rights standards, although they are clarified by the requirement that such limitations can also be justified in relation to the explicit triple test elements.

A year later in 2000 with the adoption of General Comment 14 the Committee explicitly recognise the possibility of limitations based upon grounds of 'public health' and introduce the requirements of proportionality and 'legitimate aims':

> 28. Issues of *public health* are sometimes used by States as grounds for limiting the exercise of other fundamental rights. The Committee wishes to emphasize that the Covenant's limitation clause, article 4, is primarily intended to protect the rights of individuals rather than to permit the imposition of limitations by States. Consequently a State party which, for example, restricts the movement of, or incarcerates, persons with transmissible diseases such as HIV/AIDS, refuses to allow doctors to treat persons believed to be opposed to a government, or fails to provide immunization against the community's major infectious diseases, on grounds such as national security or the preservation of public order, has the burden of justifying such serious measures in relation to each of the elements identified in article 4. Such restrictions must be in accordance with the law, including international human rights standards,

[225] ibid.

> compatible with the nature of the rights protected by the Covenant, in the *interest of legitimate aims pursued*, and strictly necessary for the promotion of the general welfare in a democratic society.[226]
>
> 29. In line with article 5.1, *such limitations must be proportional*, i.e. the least restrictive alternative must be adopted where several types of limitations are available. Even where such limitations on grounds of protecting public health are basically permitted, they should be of limited duration and subject to review.[227]

Forman notes the Committee justify bringing in such proportionality analysis on the basis of article 5.1 of ICESCR,[228] which states:

> 5.1. Nothing in the present Covenant may be interpreted as implying for any State, group or person any right to engage in any activity or to perform any act aimed at the destruction of any of the rights or freedoms recognized herein, or at their limitation to a greater extent than is provided for in the present Covenant.[229]

However, such a basis for proportionality analysis is not explicitly noted in further General Comments. Further, it is argued that article 5 was not intended as a basis for strict proportionality analysis but rather as Sepúlveda argues, 'this

226 UN CESCR General Comment No. 14 (n 135) Limitations, para. 28. The requirement of 'legitimate aims' is repeated in General Comment No. 17 (n 222) Limitations, para. 22. Emphasis added.

227 UN CESCR General Comment No. 14 (n 135) Limitations, para. 29. The requirement of 'proportionality' is repeated in General Comment No. 17 (n 222) Limitations, para. 23. Emphasis added.

228 Forman (n 84) 191.

229 ICESCR, article 5.1. See also Chapter One.

provision is in line with the general rule of interpretation that establishes that an international treaty must be interpreted in good faith and in light of its object and purpose'.[230]

Nevertheless, the inclusion of an explicit requirement of proportionality analysis within General Comment 14 can be seen as an indicator of the increasing importance attributed to the concept of proportionality in addition to the explicit requirements of the original triple test as set out in article 4.[231] Consequently, by 2009 the requirements for limitations to pursue legitimate aims and to be proportionate are firmly established practice within General Comments.[232] Moreover, the impacts of permissible limitations on CPRs, on the enjoyment of ESCRs, are also explicitly noted, for example, General Comment No. 21 Right of everyone to take part in cultural life provides:

> The Committee also wishes to stress the need to take into consideration existing international human rights standards on limitations that can or cannot be legitimately imposed on rights that are intrinsically linked to the right to take part in cultural life, such as the rights to privacy, to freedom of thought, conscience and religion, to freedom of opinion and expression, to peaceful assembly and to freedom of association.[233]

[230] Sepúlveda (n 88) 304. See also article 31 Vienna Convention on the Law of Treaties (23 May 1969). Entered into force on 27 January 1980. United Nations, Treaty Series, vol. 1155, p 331; further discussion in Chapter Five.

[231] See further discussion in Chapter Four.

[232] UN CESCR General Comment No. 21 (n 222), para. 19. 'Such limitations must pursue a legitimate aim, be compatible with the nature of this right and be strictly necessary for the promotion of general welfare in a democratic society, in accordance with article 4 of the Covenant. Any limitations must therefore be proportionate, meaning that the least restrictive measures must be taken when several types of limitations may be imposed.'

[233] UN CESCR General Comment No. 21 (n 222) para. 19.

Significantly, in 2020 in General Comment 25 on science and economic, social and cultural rights, the CESCR explicitly stated that 'limitations must respect the minimum core obligations of the right'[234] and also that 'Core obligations related to the right to participate in and to enjoy the benefits of scientific progress and its applications require States parties to [*inter alia*] Remove limitations to the freedom of scientific research that are incompatible with article 4 of the Covenant'.[235] This is an important statement as it unequivocally acknowledges that the minimum core or essential levels of ESCRs cannot be limited in any circumstances.

Finally, the latest General Comment of the CESCR, General Comment No. 26 on land and economic, social and cultural rights (2021),[236] deals with permissible limitations in para. 23, where the Committee include a number of additional doctrines and omit of one of the original key tests as provided in article 4: As one would expect, there is explicit provision that limitations must be '*determined by law*'.[237] However, the requirement that they are '*solely for the purpose of the general welfare in a democratic society*' is supplemented with the term '*public purpose*'. The clause then clarifies that 'States parties should clearly define the concepts of public purpose in law, in order to allow for judicial review',[238] thus highlighting the need for a justiciable process and procedural obligation on states to revue such ESCRs limitations. Surprisingly, the explicit requirement

---

[234] UN CESCR General Comment No. 25 (2020) on science and economic, social and cultural rights (article 15 (1) (b), (2), (3) and (4) of the International Covenant on Economic, Social and Cultural Rights) E/C.12/GC/25 (30 April 2020), B. Limitations, para. 21.

[235] CESCR, General Comment No. 25 (2020) on science and economic, social and cultural rights (article 15 (1) (b), (2), (3) and (4) of the International Covenant on Economic, Social and Cultural Rights) E/C.12/GC/25 (30 April 2020), para. 52.

[236] UN CESCR, General Comment No. 26 (n 222) para. 23.

[237] ibid. Emphasis added.

[238] ibid. Emphasis added.

that such limitations are 'compatible with the nature of these rights' is omitted.[239] Rather, attention is drawn to the fact that such restrictions on the right to housing (ie forced evictions) must be 'compatible and in conformity with the Covenant and in accordance with the general principles of *reasonableness* and *proportionality* [...], the limitation shall be necessary, in the sense that it is the least restrictive measure to fulfil the legitimate purpose'.[240] It is concerning that the explicit requirement of restrictions having to be 'compatible with the nature of these rights' isabsent . It is questionable whether compatibility with the Covenant generally is equivalent to this requirement – the former being a general obligation whereas the latter would seem to highlight the protective and essential elements of the essence of the rights themselves.

Overall, the CESCR have developed their practice and interpretation of article 4 over time. The additional requirements of *legitimacy*, *proportionality* and *reasonableness* are significant as they supplement the triple test already provided for under the Covenant and speak to the development of a 'thicker', more complex limitations regime. The inclusion of the doctrines of reasonableness, and proportionality may also be a consequence of the development of the Optional Protocol to the ICESCR (2008),[241] individual petition procedure under article 8(4) which provides a legal basis for reasonableness review in terms of individual communications:

> Article 8 Examination of communications
> 4. When examining communications under the present Protocol, the Committee shall consider the *reasonableness* of

[239] ibid para. 23.

[240] ibid.

[241] Optional Protocol to the International Covenant on Economic, Social and Cultural Rights, 2008, United Nations Treaty Series, vol. 2922, p 29. Doc. A/63/435. Entry into Force 5 May 2013, Signatories: 46. Parties: 29.

> the steps taken by the State Party in accordance with part II of the Covenant. In doing so, the Committee shall bear in mind that the State Party may adopt a range of possible policy measures for the implementation of the rights set forth in the Covenant.[242]

The question of these additional concepts is explored shortly.[243] For now, it is pertinent to examine the jurisprudence of the Committee to assess the application of article 4 within the decisions under this individual petition procedure.

3.1.2 Jurisprudence under the Optional Protocol to the International Covenant on Economic, Social and Cultural Rights 2008

Analysis of the jurisprudence of the CESCR under ICESCR Optional Protocol also indicates a developing interpretation of article 4 limitations in relation to individual petition. A textual search of all the cases under the Optional Protocol found that from 90 decisions[244] of the Committee, seven cases explicitly dealt with the question of justified limitations with reference to either 'article 4' or to 'limitations'.[245] Six of these 'adoption

[242] ibid article 8(4).

[243] See Chapter Four.

[244] Three Opinions; 11 Adoption of Views; 22 inadmissible; 54 discontinuation decisions.

[245] Search of on 'limitation(s)' and 'article 4' OHCHR Jurisprudence Database http://juris.ohchr.org, 10 July 2022, revealed seven cases under CESCR. A previous search on 6 July 2021 revealed five cases. NB: This does not include cases without explicit reference to limitations or article 4. Manually updated data 31 July 2023; March 2024. Grohmann has noted that in CESCR Communication No. 5/2015, *Ben Djazia et al v Spain*, E/C.12/61/D/5/2015 (21 July 2017), the Committee alluded to article 4 ICESCR but without explicit reference. See Nils-Hendrik Grohmann, 'Tracing the Development of the Proportionality Analysis in Relation to Forced Evictions under the ICESCR', *Human Rights Law Review* 22 (2022), 1, 6.

of views' were in the context of assessing the proportionality of limitations on housing rights in relation to evictions,[246] and one in relation to the right to health.[247] Another two cases were added manually when updating the dataset, making the total relevant cases nine.[248] It is not the intention to analyse each of these cases in detail.[249] Rather, the aim is to trace the development of the interpretation of article 4 across the jurisprudence of the Committee to date.

In the first of these cases, *S.C. and G.P. v Italy* (2019), on the right to the highest attainable standard of health, the Committee reiterate that 'article 4, is primarily intended to protect the rights of individuals rather than to permit the

[246] CESCR Communication No. 61/2018, *Lorne Joseph Walters v Belgium*, E/C.12/70/D/61/2018 (23 November 2021); CESCR Communication No. 048/2018 *Romero and Children v Spain*, E/C.12/69/D/48/2018 (21 April 2021), para. 12.4; CESCR Communication No. 54/2018 *El Ayoubi and Mohamed El Azouan Azouz v Spain*, E/C.12/69/D/54/2018 (23 March 2021), paras 11.2; 11.3; 11.4; CESCR Communication No. 085/2018 *Hakima El Goumari and Ahmed Tidli v Spain* E/C.12/69/D/85/2018 (16 March 2021), paras 8.2; 8.3; 10.1; CESCR Communication No. 052/2018 *Gómez-Limón Pardo v Spain*, E/C.12/67/D/52/2018 (14 April 2020), para. 9.4; CESCR Communication No. 37/2018, *López Albán v Spain*, E/C.12/66/D/37/2018 (29 November 2019), para. 11.1, 11.6, 11.7.

[247] CESCR Communication No. 022/2017 *S.C. and G.P. v Italy*, E/C.12/65/D/22/2017 (28 March 2019), paras 7.4; 9; 11.2.

[248] CESCR Communication No. 70/2018, *Sara Vázquez Guerreiro, D.S.V. and Y.S. V v Spain*, E/C.12/74/D/70/2018 (9 November 2023); CESCR Communication No. 226/2021 and No. 227/2021, *Hamid Saydawi and Masir Farah v Italy*, E/C.12/75/D/226/2021, E/C.12/75/D/227/2021 (13 March 2024).

[249] For detailed analysis of the early cases of the Optional Protocol and the development of review, see Sandra Liebenberg, 'Between Sovereignty and Accountability: The Emerging Jurisprudence of the United Nations Committee on Economic, Social and Cultural Rights Under the Optional Protocol' (2020) 42 *Human Rights Quarterly*, 48.

imposition of limitations by States'.[250] Further, they explicitly state the requirements of the triple test and the requirements of legitimacy and necessity. The Committee found a violation of the right to health, reasoning that the limitations in this case were not compatible with the nature of the right to health. They held that the prohibition in question 'touches upon the very substance of the right to health and goes beyond the kind of restriction that would be justified under article 4 of the Covenant'.[251] In other words, the Committee highlight the fact that certain limitations are beyond the scope of article 4, that is, those that affect the *essence* of the right – the *minimum core*.

Later that year in November 2019 *López Albán v Spain* in the Committee adopt views noting a violation of the right to housing due to forced eviction. The Committee considered 'whether the author's eviction from the apartment she was occupying constituted a violation of her right to adequate housing or whether the authorities' intervention constituted a justified limitation on her right to housing in accordance with article 4 of the Covenant'.[252] It is notable that there is no explicit analysis of whether the requirements as set out in the

[250] CESCR Communication No. 022/2017 *S.C. and G.P. v Italy*, E/C.12/65/D/22/2017 (28 March 2019), Permitted limitations to the right to the highest attainable standard of health, para. 9.

[251] ibid para. 11.2, '11.2 Restrictions to rights protected under the Covenant must comply with the limitations provided in article 4 of the Covenant. The Committee recalls that, according to article 4, restrictions must be "compatible with the nature of these rights". The Committee has found that the prohibition on withdrawing one's consent to the transfer of an embryo constitutes a violation of the right to health, as it can lead to forced medical interventions or even forced pregnancies. This prohibition touches upon the very substance of the right to health and goes beyond the kind of restriction that would be justified under article 4 of the Covenant.'

[252] CESCR Communication No. 37/2018, *López Albán v Spain*, E/C.12/66/D/37/2018 (29 November 2019), para. 11.1.

triple test have been met. Rather, the CESCR considered that the lack of a proportionality analysis 'of the legitimate objective of the eviction to its consequences for the persons evicted',[253] did not satisfy the requirements of permissible limitations as set out in article 4. They concluded:

> 11.7 The Committee therefore considers that the eviction, insofar as it was conducted without a prior assessment of the proportionality between the aim pursued by the measure and its consequences for the evicted persons, and thus without satisfying the conditions established in article 4, constituted a violation by the State party of the author's and her children's right to housing, as set forth in article 11 of the Covenant.[254]

This is the first instance where the Committee explicitly document a proportionality analysis under the Optional Protocol. In subsequent cases, we see the requirements of a proportionality test explicitly noted and expanded upon in a similar way to the attention given to proportionality found in later General Comments of the Committee. In *Gómez-Limón Pardo v Spain* (2020) we see the Committee develop a standard clause, which is then used in future cases going forwards. This includes a requirement to meet two of the three requirements of the triple test with an additional requirement that a proportionality assessment be undertaken based upon article 2(1) obligations. It also requires that an authoritative body carry out such a proportionality assessment:

> 9.4 When an eviction might result in a person's being deprived of access to adequate housing and exposed to a risk of destitution or some other violation of his or her

[253] ibid para. 11.5.
[254] ibid para. 11.7.

Covenant rights, *an obligation to analyse the proportionality of the measure arises*. This obligation flows from the interpretation of the State party's obligations under article 2 (1) of the Covenant, read in conjunction with article 11, and in accordance with the requirements of article 4. The Committee notes that the author claimed that the eviction would constitute interference with her right to adequate housing. The Committee further notes that article 4 of the Covenant stipulates the conditions under which such limitations on the enjoyment of Covenant rights are permitted. Firstly, the limitation must be *determined by law*. Secondly, it must promote the *general welfare in a democratic society*. Thirdly, it must be suited to the *legitimate* purpose cited. Fourthly, the limitation must be *necessary*, in the sense that if there is more than one measure that could reasonably be expected to serve the purpose of the limitation, the least restrictive measure must be chosen. Lastly, the benefits of the limitation in promoting the general welfare must outweigh the impacts on the enjoyment of the right being limited. The more serious the impact on the author's Covenant rights, the greater the scrutiny that must be given to the grounds invoked for such a limitation. *This analysis of the proportionality of the measure must be carried out by a judicial or other impartial and independent authority with the power to order the cessation of the violation and to provide an effective remedy. This authority must analyse whether the eviction is compatible with the Covenant, including with regard to the elements of the proportionality test required by article 4 of the Covenant as described above.*[255]

[255] CESCR Communication No. 052/2018 *Gómez-Limón Pardo v Spain*, E/C.12/67/D/52/2018 (14 April 2020), para. 9.4. Emphasis added. See also CESCR Communication No. 54/2018 *El Ayoubi and Mohamed El Azouan Azouz v Spain*, E/C.12/69/D/54/2018 (23 March 2021), paras 11.2, 11.3 and 11.4; CESCR Communication No. 085/2018 *Hakima El Goumari and Ahmed Tidli v Spain*, E/C.12/69/D/85/2018 (16 March 2021), paras 8.2, 8.3 and 10.1.

Notably in this case, 'the first and second conditions – that the limitation must be determined by law and that it must promote the general welfare in a democratic society – are in direct conformity with the wording of article 4 ICESCR.[256] However, the requirements of legitimacy, necessity and proportionality are not explicit requirements of article 4. Rather they are additional doctrine and interpretive tools to assess if the explicit requirements have been met. Moreover, 'in contrast to the normative basis adduced in *López Albán v Spain*, the Committee consider article 2(1) ICESCR as the decisive provision for testing the proportionality of an eviction',[257] with the provision to be read alongside the requirements of article 4 ICESCR. This highlights the continuing confusion/nexus between article 2(1) and article 4 as the grounds for restricting Covenant rights.

Up until this point in 2020, the evidence demonstrates that there has been, at worst, inconsistent practice or, at best, developing practice by the Committee in interpreting the basis for limitations under ICESCR.[258] Empirically, in fact, application of article 4 has been divergent – initially focussed on the 'nature' of the right, the essence or minimum core, and explicitly citing and applying the original doctrine as set out in the triple test, but more recently based upon on additional legal provisions, such as article 2(1) and/or supplementary doctrines or interpretive concepts. For example, the additional requirements of legitimacy and necessity although not unusual or innovative in a proportionality assessment[259] are new to the practice of the CESCR.

[256] Nils-Hendrik Grohmann. 'Tracing the Development of the Proportionality Analysis in Relation to Forced Evictions under the ICESCR' (2022) 22, *Human Rights Law Review* 1, 9.

[257] ibid.

[258] Cf with Grohmann's assessment of consistent practice, ibid p 9.

[259] ibid.

In 2021, in the case of *Lorne Joseph Walters v Belgium* the CESCR consider 'whether the author's eviction constituted a violation of his right to adequate housing or whether the authorities' intervention constituted a justified limitation on the right to adequate housing in accordance with article 4 of the Covenant'.[260] In their adoption of views, they use the same reasoning and wording as per the *Gómez-Limón Pardo v Spain* (2020) case,[261] to assess whether there has been a sufficient proportionality test to meet the requirements of article 4.[262] Similarly, in *Sara Vázquez Guerreiro, D.S.V. and Y.S.V. v Spain* this provision is repeated verbatim.[263]

In the most recent case of *Hamid Saydawi and Masir Farah v Italy,* the views adopted by the CESCR, are based upon the standard triple test plus a proportionality and reasonableness assessment.[264] However, a new requirement is also added to the General recommendations which provides that the State Party has a clear obligation to afford remedies including 'guarantees of non-repetition'[265] including an obligation:

> 13 (a) To ensure that its normative framework allows persons […] to challenge the decision before a judicial or other impartial and independent authority with the

[260] CESCR Communication No. 61/2018, *Lorne Joseph Walters v Belgium*, E/C.12/70/D/61/2018 (23 November 2021), para. 11.1.

[261] CESCR Communication No. *Gómez-Limón Pardo v Spain* (E/C.12/67/D/52/2018), para. 9.4. Also referenced in CESCR, General Comment 26 on Land para. 23 when discussing limitations.

[262] CESCR Communication No. 61/2018, *Lorne Joseph Walters v Belgium*, E/C.12/70/D/61/2018 (23 November 2021), para. 9.3.

[263] CESCR Communication No. 70/2018, *Sara Vázquez Guerreiro, D.S.V. and Y.S.V v Spain*, E/C.12/74/D/70/2018 (9 November 2023), General recommendations, para. 16(a). See also paras 8.2; 8.3; 8.4; 14.1 and 14.2.

[264] CESCR Communication No. 226/2021 and No. 227/2021, *Hamid Saydawi and Masir Farah v Italy*, E/C.12/75/D/226/2021, E/C.12/75/D/227/2021 (13 March 2024) paras 8.3 and 11.1.

[265] ibid para. 13.

> power to order the cessation of the violation and to provide an effective remedy so that such authorities can examine the proportionality of the measure in the light of the criteria for limiting the rights enshrined in the Covenant under the terms of article 4.[266]

This mirrors the development of provision for judicial review as found in General Comment 26 on land.[267]

Thus, having examined the views of the committee under the individual petition mechanisms of the Optional Protocol, the data would seem to indicate two main developments: first, the development of a standardised process and criteria for dealing with assessment of article 4 limitations. Second, that such an assessment includes not just the triple test as set out explicitly in article 4 but also entails both a proportionality assessment and consideration of the principle of reasonableness as set out by the Committee. The merits or drawbacks of such an approach will be considered in Chapter Four; however it should be noted, that the overwhelming majority of cases under the Optional Protocol that deal with article 4 have been in relation to article 11 and specifically the right to housing. As such, there is a question as to whether the Committee would interpret article 4 in the same way if presented with cases concerning other rights under article 11 or under other articles of the Covenant.[268]

Despite this potential shortcoming, the use of this wider criteria for assessing the lawfulness of such article 4 restrictions under the Optional Protocol, demonstrates a development in interpretation by the Committee. As such, it is necessary to examine these additional concepts in further detail to assess their usefulness but also their impact on existing doctrines within the ICESCR. Before doing so, however, it is important

[266] ibid para. 13 (a).

[267] General Comment 26, para. 23, footnote 90.

[268] Grohmann (n 256) 23.

to examine the practice of the Committee in relation to the wider performance of States, under the state periodic reporting process.

3.1.3 Concluding Observations

To gain wider insight into the assessment by the CESCR of restrictions put in place by States Parties to the Covenant, it is crucial to assess the evaluation of States Parties periodic reports by the Committee, through an analysis of their Concluding Observations. A free text search of the Concluding Observations of the Committee found 144 recommendations in 82 documents noting concern over excessive or broad restrictions to Covenant rights.[269] This is compared with only three instances where article 4 is explicitly referred to.[270] Thus, it is evident in the data that in the past the Committee has been much more likely to raise concerns generally about restrictions to ESCRs without reference to article 4, than to explicitly remind states of their obligations under article 4. In all three cases where explicit reference is made to article 4, the States are requested to ensure the restrictions in place are compatible with article 4. However, each further detailed recommendations are made. For example, in the 2014 Concluding Observations

[269] Universal Human Rights Index, http://uhri.ohchr.org Search CESCR, 'restrictions', updated 15 October 2022. The Universal Human Rights Index provides a database of all human rights recommendations and information emanating from international human rights mechanisms in the UN system: the Treaty Bodies, the Special Procedures and the Universal Periodic Review (UPR).

[270] Vietnam E/C.12/VNM/CO/2–4 (CESCR 2014) Concluding observations on the second to fourth periodic reports of Viet Nam (15 December 2014); Committee on Economic, Social and Cultural Rights, Concluding Observations on the fourth periodic report of Cameroon, E/C.12/CMR/CO/4 (25 March 2019); Concluding observations of the Committee on Economic, Social and Cultural Rights China: Hong Kong Special Administrative Region, E/C.12/1/Add.58 (21 May 2001).

on The Second to Fourth Periodic Reports of Vietnam, the CESCR express concern at overly broad limitations and:

> urges the State party to review the restrictions to the exercise of economic, social and cultural rights, as provided for in article 14 (2) of the Constitution and implementing regulations and legislation, so as to bring them into line with article 4 of the Covenant, and to ensure that they are *necessary* and *proportionate* and *do not interfere with the core minimal content* of the rights.[271]

It is notable that the Committee draw attention to the fact that the minimum core of ESCRs cannot be limited.

When the Committee considered the fourth periodic report of Cameroon in 2019, they noted their concern over restrictions on internet access 'which have constrained the exercise of economic, social and cultural rights, including the right to enjoy the benefits of scientific progress and its applications (art. 15)'.[272] Furthermore, they called upon Cameroon:

> to ensure that any limitations placed on access to the Internet are in all cases subject to careful scrutiny in order to make sure that they are *necessary* and *proportionate* to the circumstances, *temporary* and non-discriminatory, and to ensure that any Internet restrictions are compatible with article 4 of the Covenant and *provided for by law*.[273]

This example illustrates how limitations on access to information can negatively impact upon not just the enjoyment

[271] Vietnam E/C.12/VNM/CO/2–4 (CESCR 2014) Concluding observations on the second to fourth periodic reports of Viet Nam (15 December 2014), para. 8. Emphasis added.

[272] Committee on Economic, Social and Cultural Rights, Concluding Observations on the fourth periodic report of Cameroon, E/C.12/CMR/CO/4 (25 March 2019), para. 64.

[273] ibid, para. 65. Emphasis added.

of civil and political rights but also economic, social and cultural rights. However, the recommendation also reflects the additional doctrine of proportionality and necessity and does not reinforce the actual requirements of the triple test under article 4 (although it does sets out the requirement for compatibility with article 4 of the Covenant).

In the Committee's Concluding Observations on Hong Kong, it notes that any limitations on the enjoyment of article 10 protection of the family 'must be justified in relation to each element set out in article 4'.[274]

There are a number of other references to restrictions in the Concluding Observations of the Committee that do not explicitly mention article 4 itself, including a number, which refer specifically to limitations in reference to legally declared 'states of emergency' under domestic law. As noted previously, a crisis does not necessarily equate to a legal state of emergency, and, as demonstrated, article 4 limitations can apply in many kinds of crises.

In their concluding observations on Algeria the Committee recommended 'that the State party consider, based on the principles of *necessity* and *proportionality,* lifting the protracted state of emergency, in place since 1992, insofar as it has a negative effect on the enjoyment of economic, social and cultural rights in the State party (arts. 4 and 5)'.[275]

---

[274] Concluding observations of the Committee on Economic, Social and Cultural Rights China: Hong Kong Special Administrative Region, E/C.12/1/Add.58 (21 May 2001), para. 40: '40. When formulating and implementing its policies on permanent residence and split families, HKSAR is urged to give the most careful attention to all the human rights dimensions of the issue, including articles 2(2), 3 and 10 of the Covenant. The Committee reminds HKSAR that any limitations in connection with article 10 must be justified in relation to each element set out in article 4. The Committee urges HKSAR to reconsider extending the "concession" made by HKSAR following the reinterpretation of 26 June 1999.'

[275] Concluding observations of the Committee on Economic, Social and Cultural Rights, Algeria, E/C.12/DZA/CO/4 (7 June 2010), para. 23.

In the Concluding Observations on the fourth periodic report of Ecuador, the Committee note that the State must 'Ensure that the declaration of a state of emergency and its implementation are consistent with the principles of *proportionality, necessity* and other principles established by international human rights standards.'[276] This is referring to a state of emergency declared in relation to austerity measures and social protests. What is interesting is that in relation to limitations on ESCRs in this crisis they consider them under article 2(1) retrogressive measures rather than article 4.[277] Article 4 is not referred to. This supports the previously made argument regarding the confusion between article 2(1) de facto limitations and article 4 measures.

In their Concluding Observations on Sri Lanka (2010), the CESCR state their concern regarding the impact of the state of emergency and consider it to be 'hampering the full realization

[276] Concluding observations of the Committee on Economic, Social and Cultural Rights, Ecuador, E/C.12/ECU/CO/4 (14 November 2019), para. 8 (b). Emphasis added.

[277] ibid, para. 5: 'The Committee [...] is concerned about the impact of the austerity measures under the Prosperity Plan 2018–2021 and the Extended Fund Facility of the International Monetary Fund on the enjoyment of economic, social and cultural rights (article 2 (1)'; para. 6(d): 'Bear in mind that retrogressive measures are compatible with the Covenant only if they are *necessary* and *proportionate*, in the sense that the adoption of any other policy, or a failure to act, would be more detrimental to economic, social and cultural rights; the affected populations should be consulted with regard to such measures, which should be independently reviewed; the measures should remain in place only insofar as they remain necessary; they should not result in discrimination and they should mitigate inequalities that can grow in times of crisis, ensuring that the rights of disadvantaged and marginalized individuals and groups are not disproportionately affected; and they should not affect the minimum core content of the rights protected under the Covenant (open letter dated 16 May 2012 addressed to States parties in relation to economic, social and cultural rights in the context of the economic and financial crisis).' Emphasis added.

of the economic, social and cultural rights'.[278] They urge the State Party 'to consider repealing all remaining emergency regulations which jeopardize the realization of economic, social and cultural rights'.[279] Despite this acknowledgement that emergency laws are restricting ESCRs, there is no mention of article 4 requirements or a statement as to whether they consider the restrictions in conformity with the article.

In sum, having analysed the results from the dataset, it is evident that the attention given to article 4 limitations within the Concluding Observations of the Committee and the examination of periodic States Reports is minimal. Where they have commented on States Parties' use of article 4 limitations, it has most frequently been in the context of domestic states of emergency and excessive limitations on ESCRs. This limited engagement could be due to a number of factors: it could be that concerns around de facto limitations on the enjoyment of ESCRs are more likely to be the focus of discussion under article 2 obligations and the long-term monitoring of progressive realisation. It could also be that the issue of limitations has rarely been considered in any substance of depth, within the State Reports themselves. As such, it is pertinent to examine how states themselves conceive of and report on article 4 of the Covenant.

3.2 State Parties practice – an empirical analysis of article 4 within periodic reports to CESCR

Having analysed the practice of the CESCR, it is important to examine how States Parties to ICESCR understand their obligations regarding article 4 and how such parties have applied article 4 in practice. This will enable a full picture of

[278] Concluding observations of the Committee on Economic, Social and Cultural Rights, Sri Lanka, E/C.12/LKA/CO/2–4 (9 December 2010), para. 7.

[279] ibid.

how permissible limitations on ESCRs are understood and applied by States Parties to the ICESCR.

With this aim in mind, using the same methodology, a deep dive textual analysis of all 418 States Reports to CESCR[280] was undertaken. Of these periodic reports, 121 mentioned article 4 limitations in some way. A number of themes were identified: First, there was a tendency for states to repeat the text of article 4 verbatim with no specific information provided as to how they understood article 4 or if/how it had been used in practice (35 reports).[281] Second, States Parties reported application of limitations in relation to their own constitutional frameworks with a tendency to generalise limitations provisions, focusing on derogations regimes or limitations on civil and political rights, and often with no reference to limitations on ESCRs.[282] This was most prevalent in relation to 'states of emergency', which is discussed later. This reinforces the findings of Müller's earlier research that 'all too often, states list possibilities to limit or derogate from civil and political rights in their reports on Article 4 only'.[283]

Significantly, several state reports contained an explicit statement that in a general context, no limitations had been applied to ESCRs, nine in total.[284] A strong example of

---

[280] Dataset up to and including the CESCR 71st session, March 22.

[281] For example, see CESCR State Report Hong Kong – China 2020 (due 2019) E/C.12/CHN-HKG/4, para. 45; CESCR State Report China: Report of the Hong Kong Special Administrative Region of the People's Republic Of China, E/1990/5/Add.43, para. 39; CESCR State Report Zimbabwe 1995, E/1990/5/Add.28, para. 12.

[282] For example, see CESCR State Report Turkmenistan 2010, E/C.12/TKM/1, paras 40–2; CESCR State Report Kazakhstan 2009, para. 138–9.

[283] Müller (n 2) 567.

[284] CESCR State Report 2001 New Zealand, E/1990/6/Add.33, para. 729; CESCR State Report 2011 New Zealand, E/C.12/NZL/3, paras 777 and 778; CESCR State Report 2001 UK Islands, E/C.12/4/Add.7, para. 428; CESCR State Report 2008 UK Islands, E/C.12/GBR/5/

this position can be seen in the 1995 State Report of the Dominican Republic, which provides:

> Articles 4 and 5: Limitations on the enjoyment of the rights laid down in the Covenant
> 32. Because of the intrinsic nature of the economic, social and cultural rights of the human person, it is difficult to conceive of any type of restrictions on them either in legislation or in practice. The intrinsic nature of these rights has been fully understood by the Dominican State, which has not established any limitations on their enjoyment either in its constitutional principles or in positive law.[285]

Significantly, Armenia's 1998 report documents permissible restrictions to civil and political rights during times of emergency while stating that '[r]estrictions of economic, social and cultural human rights are unacceptable under Armenian law'.[286]

Moreover, some states reported a general rule of no limitations but noted specific exceptions to this rule. For example, Mexico's 1998 report states that there can be no

Add.1, para. 66; CESCR State Report 2005 Morocco, E/1994/104/Add.29 (17 January 2005), para. 86; CESCR State Report 2012 Austria, E/C.12/AUT/4, para. 38; CESCR State Report 2013 Paraguay, E/C.12/PRY/4, para. 47; CESCR State Report 2013 Vietnam, E/C.12/VNM/2–4, para. 86; CESCR State Report Dominican Republic 1995, E/1990/6/Add.7 (5 March 1995), para. 32 with explicit reference to 'nature' of ESCRS as preventing limitations. In addition, CESCR State Report 2008 UK E/C.12/GBR/5, para. 205 notes that under article 4 the United Kingdom has 'Nothing to report under this article.'

285 CESCR Second periodic reports submitted by States Parties under articles 16 and 17 of the Covenant, Addendum, Dominican Republic (15 March 1995) E/1990/6/Add.7, para. 32.

286 CESCR, 'Armenia: Initial reports submitted by States parties under articles 16 and 17 of the Covenant' (9 December 1998) E/1990/5/Add.36, para. 53. See also paras 49–52. See discussion of emergencies later.

limitations on ESCRs save for article 8 (trade unions), based on their existing reservation entered when the State Party ratified the ICESCR.[287] Another example can be seen in the 1981 State Report of Iraq to the CESCR, which states that:

> Article 4: Limitations imposed on the application of articles 10 to 12
> No legislative, administrative or judicial limitations are imposed on the application of articles 10 to 12. On the contrary, Iraq is endeavouring to promote the exercise of the rights specified in these articles by removing all obstacles hindering their full enjoyment within the limits stipulated in the Covenant.[288]

It is notable that they identify particular ESCRs that cannot be limited – the right to protection for the family, the right to an adequate standard of living and right to health only. This may suggest a hierarchy of ESCRs whereby basic 'survival' rights and protection of the vulnerable are deemed so fundamental they cannot be limited in anyway. Müller acknowledges that limitations may be interpreted differently depending on the

[287] CESCR State Report 1998 Mexico E/1994/104/Add.18, para. 52 as noted in a reservation to the ICESCR at time of ratification. Note also, that article 8 is subject to specific limitations unlike the other substantive rights contained in the ICECSR.

[288] Implementation of the International Covenant on Economic, Social and Cultural Rights Reports submitted In accordance with Council resolution 1988 (LX) by States Parties to the Covenant concerning rights covered by articles 10 to 12, Iraq E/1980/6/Add.14 (27 January 1981). NB In their most recent report of 2021, the provision is much less specific and merely reiterates the article provision, 'The States Parties to the Covenant recognize that the State may not lawfully limit the enjoyment of the rights stipulated under the present Covenant save insofar as such limitation is compatible with the nature of these rights and solely for the purpose of promoting the common good in a democratic society' (Fifth periodic report submitted by Iraq under articles 16 and 17 of the Covenant, due in 2020, E/C.12/IRQ/5 [20 August 2021], para. 127).

nature of ESCRs concerned, For example, she notes that subsistence rights are the most important, as they are 'necessary for the very survival of people (for example, the right to basic food, a basic level of health care, clothing and basic shelter)', whereas those 'which are not as vital for the immediate survival of people, such as the rights related to trade unions (Article 8 ICESCR), or the right to take part in cultural life (Article 15 ICESCR)'[289] may be limited. In fact, the right to form and join a trade union contained in article 8 has its own provision specific limitation written into the text of the clause and so is distinct from other rights contained within the Covenant as a matter of law.[290]

Other states make an explicit statement that there *are limits on ESCRs*, in some instances noting limitations on specific rights. For example, Kosovo holds that restrictions on the rights to social protection, health, education and housing can be imposed for the benefit of the general welfare in a democracy society, but have not been put in place as yet.[291]

Importantly, there is also acknowledgement that the *minimum essential levels of ESCRs cannot be limited* (acknowledgement of inviolable minimum core), although this was only found explicitly in two States Parties' reports; Switzerland's report explains that article 36 of its Constitution lays out its system of limitations, in line with article 4. In particular, article 36 provides that *inter alia*, 'The essential content of the fundamental rights is inviolable'.[292] Similarly, the Lichtenstein 2004 report provides that:

[289] Müller (n 2) 584.

[290] Articles 8 (1)(a) and 8(1)(c); article 8(2) ICESCR.

[291] CESCR, 'Kosovo (Serbia): Document submitted by the United Nations Interim Administration Mission in Kosovo under articles 16 and 17 of the Covenant', E/C.12/UNK/1 (15 January 2008), para. 114.

[292] CESCR, 'Switzerland: Second and third periodic reports of States parties under articles 16 and 17 of the Covenant', E/C.12/CHE/2–3 (17 July 2009), para. 107.

> Article 4: Limitations on the rights guaranteed
> 23. [...] Fundamental rights may only be limited, however, if the limitation fulfils the following four conditions: – It must be based on legislation; – It must be justified by a prevailing public interest; – It must respect the principle of proportionality; – It may not violate the core content of the fundamental right.[293]

3.2.1 States Parties practice re article 4 in crises

As regards permissible limitations during a crisis, many States equated article 4 of ICESCR with a general derogation clause or trigger clause to enable a state of emergency akin to that of article 4 of the ICCPR. States Parties often reported on general limitations and derogations as provided for under their constitutional law in relation to civil and political rights, rather than in relation to the rights provided by the ICESCR. Of the 418 states reports in the dataset, in total, there were 33 states reports that reported on the possibility to invoke article 4 limitations due to a state of emergency.[294] Of these only eight

[293] Implementation of the International Covenant on Economic, Social and Cultural Rights, Initial reports submitted by States Parties under articles 16 and 17 of the Covenant, Addendum, Liechtenstein, E/1990/5/Add.66 (27 October 2004), para. 23.

[294] CESCR State Report 1996 Peru, E/1990/5/Add.29, paras 114–22; CESCR State Report 1997 Ireland, E/1990/5/Add.34, para. 94; CESCR State Report 1998 Armenia, E/1990/5/Add.36, paras 50–53; CESCR State Report 1998 Mongolia, E/1994/104/Add.21, para. 19; CESCR State Report 1998 Portugal, E/1994/104/Add.20, para. 73; CESCR State Report 1999 Kyrgyzstan, E/1990/5/Add.42, para. 13–14; CESCR State Report 2000 Croatia, E/1990/5/Add.46, paras 41–4; CESCR State Report 2000 Nepal, E/1990/5/Add.45, para. 88; CESCR State Report 2000 Trinidad, E/1990/6/Add.30, paras 43–5; CESCR State Report 2001 Czech, E/1990/5/Add.47, paras 161–6; CESCR State Report 2003 Kuwait, E/1990/5/Add.57, paras

specifically considered ESCRs in times of emergency: Guyana simply repeats the provisions of article 4.[295] Moldova provides that since the Covenant entered into force, 'exceptional circumstances have not been invoked'.[296]

More commonly, there is recognition of article 4 limitations on ESCRs 'in times of emergency' generally or in relation to legal 'states of emergency/exception'. For example, Nepal holds that ESCRs can be restricted in times of public emergency:

> Article 4: Limitations on economic, social and cultural rights
> 174. The enjoyment of economic, social and cultural rights can be subjected by law to certain limitations for the purpose of promoting general welfare, particularly in times of public emergency. […] where a grave crisis

66–8; CESCR State Report 2004 China, E/1990/5/Add.59, paras 823–6; CESCR State Report 2004 Slovenia, E/1990/5/Add.62, paras 53–4; CESCR State Report 2006 Macedonia, E/C.12/MKD/1, paras 98–104; CESCR State Report 2006 Nepal, E/C.12/NPL/2, paras 110–13; CESCR State Report 2009 Algeria, E/C.12/DZA/4, paras 148–52; CESCR State Report 2012 Czech Republic, E/C.12/CZE/2 para. 67; CESCR State Report 2012 Nepal, E/C.12/NPL/3, paras 174–6; CESCR State Report 2013 Armenia, E/C.12/ARM/2–3, paras 23–4; CESCR State Report 2014 Guyana, E/C.12/GUY/2–4, paras 119–120; CESCR State Report 2017 CaboVerde, E/C.12/CPV/1, paras 22–5; CESCR State Report 2019 Czechia, E/C.12/CZE/3, paras 33–4; CESCR State Report 2000 Algeria, E/1990/6/Add.26, para. 46; CESCR State Report 2006 Tajikistan, E/C.12/TJK/1, para. 124; CESCR State Report 2009 Chad, E/C.12/TCD/3, paras 63–5; CESCR State Report 2003_Moldova, E/1990/5/Add.52, paras 152–4; CESCR State Report 2013 Chile, E/C.12/CHL/4, paras 21–2; CESCR State Report 2013 Gambia, E/C.12/GMB/1, para. 63; CESCR State Report 2013 Sudan, E/C.12/SDN/2, para. 106; CESCR State Report 2013 Venezuela, E/C.12/VEN/3, paras 280–3; CESCR State Report 2016_Netherlands, E/C.12/NLD/6, para. 223; CESCR State Report 2021 Palestine, E/C.12/PSE/1, paras 42–8.

[295] CESCR State Report 2014 Guyana, E/C.12/GUY/2–4, para. 119.

[296] CESCR State Report 2003 Moldova, E/1990/5/Add.52, para. 154.

> arises in regard to the sovereignty or integrity of Nepal or the security of any part thereof, whether by war, external invasion, armed rebellion or extreme economic disarray.[297]

Para. 175 further confirms that although the right to health, education, culture and social security can be limited, they cannot be derogated from.[298] Similarly, the 2019 CESCR State Report of Czechia states that 'no right can be completely denied' even in such emergency situations.[299]

Another example is seen in the 2017 State Report of Cabo Verde, which states that:

> 25. The ratification of the International Covenant on Economic, Social and Cultural Rights binds the Cabo Verdean State, charging it with the obligation to comply with it, in accordance with article 12 of the Constitution. As such, the basic law enshrines broad support for economic and social rights, only allowing, in exceptional and well-defined situations, restrictions on fundamental human rights.[300]

As noted previously, Alston and Quinn assert that empirically governments most commonly seek to limit economic and social rights by reference to concerns for national security, as this appears to be borne out by the data gathered. 'Such reasons can legitimately be invoked only in so far as they are genuinely

[297] Implementation of the International Covenant on Economic, Social and Cultural Rights, Third periodic reports submitted by States Parties under articles 16 and 17 of the Covenant, Nepal, E/C.12/NPL/3 (29 October 2012), para. 174.

[298] ibid.

[299] CESCR State Report 2019 Czechia, E/C.12/CZE/3, para. 34.

[300] CESCR State Report 2017 CaboVerde, E/C.12/CPV/1, para. 25.

synonymous with "the general welfare"' in society.[301] However, the data illustrated that the grounds for such limitations were often not clear and referred to the ICCPR principles such as necessity, proportionality[302] or grounds such as public order,[303] rather than article 4 ICESCR grounds including 'general welfare'.

In addition to the eight reports where ESCRs were considered as part of an emergency regime, four states reported de facto limitations on ESCRs due to resource constraints or due to conflict: In Chad's 2009 report they note that:

> 63. The Chadian State conforms to the spirit of the provisions of articles 4 and 5. Only in situations of extreme emergency or when the Government is facing serious difficulties that prevent it from ensuring the enjoyment of economic, social and cultural rights in a normal manner can limitations be introduced.
>
> 64. The main constraint in implementing the Covenant is the fact that the State often lacks the necessary resources to respond promptly to the concerns of citizens.[304]

In the case of Venezuela, the report states that despite the serve economic crisis and a shortage of basic foodstuffs, 'a state of emergency was not decreed on the grounds that human rights were more important than any political consideration'.[305]

---

[301] Alston and Quinn (n 82) 202.

[302] CESCR State Report 2004 China, E/1990/5/Add.59, para. 826.

[303] CESCR State Report 2013 Armenia, E/C.12/ARM/2–3, para. 23; CESCR State Report 2003 Moldova, E/1990/5/Add.52, para. 152.

[304] CESCR State Report 2009 Chad, E/C.12/TCD/3, paras 63–4. See similar in CESCR State Report 2013 Gambia, E/C.12/GMB/1, para. 63.

[305] CESCR State Report 2013 Venezuela, E/C.12/VEN/3, para. 283. In this case it is questionable as to whether declaring a state of emergency

In the periodic report of the State of Palestine, they provide that despite the occupation, 'Palestine has taken no action aimed at restricting the rights enshrined in the Covenant'.[306] However they state that the 'unlawful occupation, and its systematic and widespread violations of international law in the Occupied Palestinian Territory prevent the Palestinian people from exercising their rights as guaranteed under international law, including the economic, social and cultural rights enshrined in the Covenant'.[307]

In the Algerian State Report they note that although:

> The measures taken under the state of emergency in no way affect the implementation of the International Covenant on Economic, Social and Cultural Rights, [...] terrorism has been one of the main factors impeding the implementation of the Covenant. Terrorist criminals, [...] have also destroyed economic, cultural and administrative infrastructure and hospitals.[308]

These examples highlight the issue previously raised of the tension between de facto limitations, article 2(1) resource questions and article 4.

As illustrated by the previously discussed data, overall, the reports evidence diverse practice within States Parties to the Covenant and little coherence in terms of an understanding or application of limitations to ESCRs under article 4 in general. Moreover, the data indicates that if restrictions are put in place, states do so in times of crisis. Such a 'state of emergency' was oft defined by States Parties *inter alia* as including war, siege, disaster, a state of martial law, mass disturbance or

---

and invoking article 4 might have been helpful in ensuring distribution of food to the most vulnerable.

306 CESCR State Report 2021 Palestine, E/C.12/PSE/1, para. 46.

307 ibid, paras 46–8.

308 CESCR State Report 2000 Algeria, E/1990/6/Add.26, para. 46.

state of alert. Significantly, both economic crisis ('extreme economic dismay')[309] and public health crisis ('epidemics')[310] were included. Additionally, whether that crisis is an armed conflict, disaster, economic or public health crisis, states tend to utilise article 4 as a general 'emergency' clause. However, it is important to note that not all contexts where article 4 can be engaged constitute a legal 'state of emergency'. For example, a situation of protracted armed conflict is not necessarily synonymous with a legal state of emergency.[311] Consequently, the data is significant in that it points to a lack of understanding of permissible limitations under the ICESCR, equating limitations of ESCRs under ICESCR, with derogation regimes focussed on suspension of CPRs in an emergency paradigm or state of exception.

3.2.2 Diversity and lack of continuity in State Parties practice – why?

There are a number of factors that could influence States Parties' practice in the application of article 4: practice could be diverse due to a lack of understanding of requirements of article 4 itself and in the absence of minimal guidance by the CESCR; It could be due to due to lack of focus on ESCRs generally and the prevalence of CPs in national systems and the international institutional human rights bodies or it could be due to a lack of understanding of reporting obligations. In 2009, the CESCR introduced new reporting guidelines in parallel with the reform of the UN Treaty Body Reporting Procedures.[312]

---

309 CESCR State Report, Nepal, E/C.12/NPL/3, 2 (9 October 2012), para. 174.

310 CESCR State Report 2003 Moldova, E/1990/5/Add.52, paras 152–3.

311 CCPR, General Comment No. 29 States of Emergency (Article 4), CCPR/C/21/Rev.1/Add.11 (31 August 2001), para. 3.

312 See Committee on Economic, Social and Cultural Rights, Guidelines on Treaty-specific Documents to Be Submitted by States Parties Under

These replaced the previous general guidelines,[313] in order 'to take into account the harmonized guidelines on reporting under the international human rights treaties (HRI/GEN/2/Rev.5), as well as the evolving practice of the Committee in relation to the application of the Covenant, as reflected in its concluding observations, general comments and statements'.[314] This change in reporting procedures could have impacted on practice as the new harmonised reporting procedure requires states to submit one common core document with:

> information on the status of all of the main international human rights treaties. [...] It should include information on:
>
> (c) Derogations, restrictions, or limitations. Where States have restricted, limited or derogated from the provisions of any of the treaties to which they are a party, the common core document should include information explaining the scope of such derogations, restrictions or limitations; the circumstances justifying them; and the timeframe envisaged for their withdrawal.[315]

Articles 16 and 17 of the International Covenant on Economic, Social and Cultural Rights, E/C.12/2008/2 (24 March 2009).

313 Committee on Economic, Social and Cultural Rights, Revised general guidelines regarding the form and contents of reports to be submitted by States Parties under articles 16 and 17 of the International Covenant on Economic, Social and Cultural Rights: note by the Secretary-General, E/C.12/1991/1 (17 June 1991).

314 Committee on Economic, Social and Cultural Rights, (n 312) para. 3.

315 Compilation of Guidelines on the Form and Content of Reports to Be Submitted by States Parties to the International Human Rights Treaties, Report of the Secretary-General, HRI/GEN/2/Rev.6 (3 June 2009), 2 General framework for the protection and promotion of human rights, C. Acceptance of international human rights norms, para. 40(c). See also D. Legal framework for the protection of human rights at the national level, para.

Further, the Annex Guidelines on Treaty-Specific Documents to Be Submitted by States Parties Under Articles 16 and 17 of The International Covenant on Economic, Social and Cultural Rights provide no further guidance noting simply, '14. See paragraph 40 (c) of the harmonized guidelines on a common core document.'[316] As such, States Parties may over generalise in their reporting on permissible limitations or indeed focus on CPRs as often perceived as primary rights as noted above. Conversely however, this clear reporting guidance could also have resulted in more States reporting on limitations generally, especially given that prior to 1991 article 4 was not included in the reporting guidelines for States Parties to the ICESCR, meaning that some states did not include any information in relation to limitations on the covenant rights.[317] As noted, the current data shows that roughly 29 per cent of the sample (121/ 418 reports) included some reference to article 4 limitations but the quality of information provided varies widely.

Another significant reason as to why there may be diverse state practice in the application of article 4 could be due to

---

42 'States should set out the specific legal context for the protection of human rights in the country. In particular, information should be provided on:

(a) Whether, and if so, which of the rights referred to in the various human rights instruments are protected either in the constitution, a bill of rights, a basic law, or other national legislation and, if so, what provisions are made for derogations, restrictions or limitations and in what circumstances;'.

[316] ibid, Annex Guidelines on Treaty-Specific Documents to Be Submitted by States Parties Under Articles 16 and 17 of the International Covenant on Economic, Social and Cultural Rights, B. Part of the treaty-specific document submitted to the Committee relating to general provisions of the Covenant, para. 14. See also Committee on Economic, Social and Cultural Rights, E/C.12/2008/2 (24 March 2009), para. 14.

[317] Revised general guidelines regarding the form and contents of reports to be submitted by States Parties under articles 16 and 17 of the International Covenant on Economic, Social and Cultural Rights, E.C/12/1991/1 (17 June 1991). See also Müller (n 2) 566.

conceptual confusion between article 4 permissible limitations and article 2(1) regarding progressive realisation. As noted previously, in doctrinal terms there is a lack of clarity as to how these two provisions should be interpreted in light of one another.[318] In States Parties practice this conceptual confusion is borne out through recognition of the overlap between article 2(1) resources and article 4 limitations. For example, States noted that often limitations were due to resource constraints rather than intentional legal restriction of ESCRs: El Salvador note in their 1995 report that despite no formal limitations on ESCRs 'limited implementation within the principle of effective progression, is imposed by limitations in resources'.[319] Honduras (1998) noted that structural adjustment measures and impact on economy had practically restricted rights.[320] Post-financial crisis, this conceptual confusion has been further complicated by the tendency to permit some retrogressive measures under article 2(1) in 'states of emergency', rather than examine such issues as a matter under article 4.[321]

3.3 Limitations to ESCRs within the UN Charter-based human rights procedures

Lastly, in addition to examining and analysing the practice of the CESCR and States Parties to the ICESCR a further empirical examination was undertaken to ascertain if limitations to ESCRs had been examined under any of the UN Charter mechanisms such as HRC Special Procedures and the HRC UPR. The rationale for a supplementary wider analysis of UN Office of the High Commissioner for Human Rights (OHCHR) documents was to examine if such mechanisms had considered limitations on ESCRs in general or in relation to

[318] See discussion in Chapter Five.

[319] El Salvador State Report to CESCR 1995, E/1990/5/Add.25, para. 28.

[320] Honduras, State Report to CESCR 1998, E/1990/5/Add.40, para. 36.

[321] See Chapter Two discussion on economic crisis.

specific treaty obligations under ICESCR and if so, to consider what insights this might offer to the overall analysis of practice.

Using the Universal Human Rights Index (UHRI),[322] a free text search of all UN 'Special Procedures' documentation found no references or discussion of limitations on ESCRs or mention of article 4 of ICESCR.[323] The only relevant finding was in a Report of the Special Rapporteur in the field of cultural rights on her visit to Botswana. This was in relation to the UDHR, as Botswana have not ratified ICESCR.[324] She notes:

> The Special Rapporteur understands the concerns expressed by the Government regarding the need to protect its rich biodiversity and its policy to ensure the economic transition of local communities through their participation in tourism activities. She recommends, however, that the Government fully abide by its obligation to respect and protect cultural rights when tailoring these policies. [...] In accordance with article 29 of the Universal Declaration on Human Rights, limitations to cultural rights shall be determined by law solely for the purpose of securing due recognition and respect for the rights and freedoms of others and meeting the just requirements of morality, public order and the general welfare in a democratic society. Any limitations must be proportionate, that is, the least restrictive

[322] Universal Human Rights Index (UHRI) https://uhri.ohchr.org/en

[323] Search undertaken on 27 July 2022 across all 'Special Procedures' (44 in total). Limitations were mentioned in 89 recommendations/observations found in 68 documents across 29 mechanisms. None of these pertained to ESCRs bar the mention under the UDHR stated previously. Search term 'article 4' also found no relevant recommendations, observations in relation to ICESCR (74 recommendations/observations in 66 documents across 22 mechanisms).

[324] Report of the Special Rapporteur in the field of cultural rights on her visit to Botswana, A/HRC/31/59/Add.1 (SR Cultural rights 2016), para. 3.

measures must be taken when several types of limitations may be imposed.[325]

In conclusion, it is evident that Special Procedures have not dealt with permissible limitations to ESCRs in any specific substantive way.

The same research method was used to undertake a free text search of the UN HRC UPR.[326] Again, the search term 'limitations' found no documents relevant to permissible limitations of ESCRs or the ICESCR.[327] The only relevant finding was a recommendation by Venezuela regarding de facto limitations caused by the economic blockade on Cuba. They urged Cuba to 'confront the limitations imposed by the blockade'.[328] Similarly, a search for 'article 4' also found no UPR recommendations, observations in relation to ICESCR.[329]

Finally, it is also interesting to note that despite conceptual confusion in state practice, and the recent instruction by the CESCR to read article 4 and article 2(1) in conjunction with one another, a search using the term 'progressive realisation' within both Special Procedures and the UPR, found no overlap between consideration of article 2(1) progressive realisation, maximum available resources and article 4 limitations.[330]

[325] ibid para. 88.

[326] Search UHRI, 27 July 22, search term 'UPR'.

[327] 111 recommendations/observations found in 94 documents within the UPR.

[328] A/HRC/24/16 (UPR 2013) Report of the Working Group on the Universal Periodic Review Cuba, Recommendation 170.201. (Venezuela); See also paras 38, 74, 78, 84.

[329] In total, 84 recommendations/observations were found from 57 documents within the UPR that referred to 'article 4' but none in relation to ESCRs.

[330] In total, 11 recommendations/observations from 11 documents under UPR were found regarding progressive realisation but none in relation to article 4; 33 recommendations/observations from 26 documents among 8 Special Procedures were found which mentioned progressive realisation but none in relation to article 4.

3.4 Concluding remarks

In sum, this overview of practice by the CESCR, States Parties to the Covenant and the wider practice of UN OHCHR mechanisms has demonstrated a lack of clarity surrounding the scope application and understanding of article 4 ICESCR. While the Committee have developed their legal test and interpretation of article 4, especially under the Optional Protocol, and to some extent within the General Comments, the basis for the legal test and which principles and doctrines should take priority remains imprecise. Additionally in the examination of States Parties reports, article 4 is rarely examined in any depth. This could reflect the lack of engagement by States Parties themselves with article 4 as well as the confusion over the requirements of article 4 as evidenced in the empirical data. The diversity of understanding of permissible limitations generally is strongly evidenced by the review.

The following chapter will therefore examine in detail the newly developing legal framework for interpreting limitations under the Covenant including the additional doctrines of proportionality and reasonableness.

FOUR

Evaluating the Interpretation and Application of Article 4 by the CESCR: A Burgeoning Framework

Having examined the interpretation and application of article 4 in a general context and in relation to varying crises it is clear that there is an increasingly complex framework developing for assessing permissible limitations under the ICESCR. In addition, based upon the analysis of the empirical data, it would seem the CESCR may be moving to a position whereby their interpretation of article 4 is based upon increasing similarity with limitations assessment under the ICCPR and a 'state of exception' model designed for civil and political rights, rather than the explicit requirements of ICESCR article 4 itself. The introduction of additional requirements, other than those noted explicitly in article 4, would also initially seem to support such a position. This raises the question as to whether a synergistic model is optimum for the protection of and promotion of ESCRs or indeed, whether such a move threatens to limit ESCRs in a more expansive way than previously. As noted by Warwick:

> The level of States' obligations during [...] crises appears to have been reduced. The similarity of those minimal tests to the derogations clauses found in other treaties is concerning. It moves the ICESCR towards incorporating

> the same flexible approaches which are found in the ICCPR, while neglecting to acknowledge the significant degree of flexibility which is already to be found in the ICESCR.[331]

Moreover, the increasing complexity and additional doctrines applied also raise the question of authenticity and legitimacy, considering the requirement to interpret the text of the Covenant in conformity with the Vienna Convention on the Law of Treaties (1969).[332]

In order to assess whether this is indeed the case, it is necessary to examine in further depth the additional doctrines of reasonableness and proportionality and crucially to examine how the CESCR understand and apply these concepts, alongside the existing doctrines provided for under the Covenant. As Young notes, there are a plethora of principles/concepts within legal guarantees for economic, social and cultural rights, which 'all beg a kind of reasoned assessment of what might be considered adequate, appropriate, available, or attainable, in context'.[333] These include article 2 concepts: progressive realisation, maximum available resources and minimum core, and article 4 limitations principles: determined by law, compatible with the nature of ESCRs and promotion of general welfare. However, in relation to assessing limitations on ESCRs, we now also find reasonableness review and proportionality. In particular, the addition of concepts such as 'reasonableness' and the related concept of 'proportionality' would appear to add to the burgeoning conceptual framework for evaluating lawful restrictions.

331 Warwick (n 151) 263.

332 See forthcoming discussion in Chapter Five.

333 Katherine Young, 'Proportionality, Reasonableness, and Economic and Social Rights' in Vicki C. Jackson and Mark Tushnet (eds), *Proportionality: New Frontiers, New Challenges* (CUP 2017) 221–247, 248.

4.1 Reasonableness

The concept of reasonableness though is not singularly defined. There are a number of differing interpretations of what 'reasonableness review' entails, not least those that deny any definition of a minimum core content for ESCRs. For example, in the case of the South African Constitutional Court reasonableness review has been applied to substantive economic and social rights without recognition of any independent substantive minimum core or minimum threshold of economic and social rights.[334] In the Court's interpretation of reasonableness, 'the interpretation of the right's content is collapsed in an incremental and context-driven inquiry'.[335] Such an interpretation has been highly criticised as the 'refusal to define content, allows reasonableness review to take place in "a normative vacuum"'.[336] Thus, it does not protect a basic minimum standard for those affected. Nor does it contribute to universal understanding of minimum standards for such rights (or help to identify the wider scope of the substantive right in question).

Bilchitz argues that reasonableness review can be a useful tool but only if applied to the wider scope of a right, once a minimum core has been defined.[337] Similarly, Landau argues that the minimum core 'should be applied in conjunction with proportionality analysis',[338] as in the case of the Colombian Constitutional Court which uses the 'vital minimum' concept

[334] ibid 262.

[335] ibid 261. See also *Grootboom*.

[336] ibid 262.

[337] David Bilchitz, *Poverty and Fundamental Rights: The Justification and Importance of Socio-Economic Rights* (OUP 2007) 183–97.

[338] David Landau, 'The Promise of a Minimum Core Approach: The Colombian Model for Judicial Review of Austerity Measures' in Aoife Nolan (ed), *Economic and Social Rights After the Global Financial Crisis* (CUP 2014) 267–98.

(similar to that of the minimum core) to give substance to the right in question. He notes:

> Proportionality review and the minimum core did not appear to be viewed by the Court as antagonistic concepts. Instead, they were seen as complementary and as playing distinct roles; the minimum core was critical in interpreting the socio-economic rights at issue, giving them clearer content by requiring prioritisation of the interests of the poor. Proportionality was then used at a subsequent stage in order to compare the infringement on the socio-economic rights with the government's justification.[339]

Consequently, in Colombia, during the economic crisis, permissible limitations were assessed 'in light of the imperatives of the vital minimum, and proportionality and the vital minimum were seen as compatible instruments carrying out separate functions'.[340] Crucially, 'the adoption of the minimum core approach would not prevent an inquiry into justifiable limitations, […] but it would 'create[s] a more rights-supportive focus'.[341] This model of interpretation would also support the interpretation of the CESCR and ensure the legal obligation, as provided under the Covenant, that the minimum core of ESCRs cannot be limited under any circumstances. Consequently, it is argued that this interpretation of reasonableness is the only way to comply with the requirements of article 4 as well as the requirements of art 2 and specific rights provisions contained within the ICESCR.

339 ibid 284.

340 ibid 268.

341 Young (n 333) 255.

4.2 Proportionality

While proportionality and reasonableness appear to be similar concepts, there are, in fact, a number of important differences: although both concepts are used to justify decisions in terms of limitations on rights, proportionality is more commonly used in relation to civil and political rights, 'in their negative dimension',[342] whereas reasonableness is associated with ESCRs.[343] Given the acceptance of civil and political rights as justiciable, it is not surprising that proportionality tests have developed within many regional and domestic human rights systems and usually consist of several components, to be considered,

> once a *prima facie* infringement of a […] right has been found. (1) First, did the infringement further a legitimate aim? (2) Second, was the measure necessary? In the most rigorous version of this test, the measure is necessary if and only if there are no alternative, less restrictive means. (3) Third, do the benefits of the measure outweigh the costs imposed on the rights-bearer?[344]

However, such a process is more suited to assessing 'individual communication[s]',[345] as reflected in the individual petition jurisprudence of the CESCR. Reasonableness review on the other hand, has been viewed as a more general 'one stage test',[346] to be applied more widely.

---

342 ibid 258.

343 ibid 250, 258; Grohmann (n 256) 3.

344 Young (n 333) 257.

345 Grohmann (n 256) 4. See also Bruce Porter, 'Reasonableness and Article 8(4)' in Malcolm Langford, Bruce Porter, Rebecca Brown and Julieta Rossi (eds), *The Optional Protocol to the International Covenant on Economic, Social and Cultural Rights: A Commentary* (PULP 2016) 173.

346 Gardbaum, 'Positive and Horizontal Rights: Proportionality's Next Frontier or a Bridge Too Far?' in Vicki C. Jackson and Mark Tushnet (eds), *Proportionality: New Frontiers, New Challenges* (CUP 2017) 221, 236.

4.3 The CESCR use of reasonableness and proportionality

As such and given the varied interpretation and application of 'reasonableness review' and its relationship with proportionality, it is important to understand how the CESCR view 'reasonableness' and 'proportionality' when applying it within their jurisprudence and more widely in their practice in relation to article 4 limitations. 'Neither the Covenant nor the Optional Protocol provides much textual guidance on the definition of the principles of proportionality and reasonableness.'[347] However, Young argues that proportionality was introduced by the Committee, as a response to the economic crisis in Europe, though this was as a principle, rather than proportionality as a process of specific analysis. Such an approach 'delinks proportionality as *principle* and proportionality analysis as a structured *doctrine*, and connects the principle of proportionality within broader standards of reasonableness'.[348] Young contends that this form of 'indirect proportionality' gives 'substance to standards of "reasonableness," "appropriate measures," and "progressive realization … according to maximum available resources"'.[349] Hence, Young argues that proportionality 'can be understood to be a subset of reasonableness'.[350] Similarly to Young, Liebenberg argues that 'the Committee does not draw a sharp distinction between the concepts of reasonableness and proportionality, appearing to view proportionality as a species of reasonableness review'.[351]

As Young notes, this thesis is reflected in the Letter by Committee on Economic, Social and Cultural Rights to States Parties to the covenant (as discussed in Chapter Two), calling for all policies confronting the economic crisis to, 'be

[347] Grohmann (n 256) 3.
[348] Young (n 333) 250.
[349] ibid 249.
[350] ibid 256.
[351] Liebenberg (n 249) 69, footnote 122.

necessary and proportionate, in the sense that the adoption of any other policy, or a failure to act, would be more detrimental to economic, social and cultural rights'.[352] Young calls this combination of proportionality and reasonableness, 'proportionality inflected reasonableness'.[353]

Zysset and Scherz argue that the development of a proportionality assessment by the CESCR confers legitimacy and legal authority (as for a body to hold legitimate authority there must be a clear procedure).[354] Moreover, they believe it is a procedure, which 'could improve the normative legitimacy of the Committees specific practice'.[355] Similar to Young, they recognise that there are 'specificities of proportionality in the field of ESC rights' both in general and in terms of the practice of the CESCR. However, they contend that the CESCR proportionality review should be considered in relation to the entire scope of a right but *especially* to the minimum core. Proportionality, they contend, 'will best operate, in particular with respect to "non-retrogressive" cases where core minimum obligations are at stake. These cases depict a situation where there is *a prima facie* violation of the provision'.[356]

Yet, this analysis fails to consider the existing legal framework under the Covenant for assessing non-retrogression and resource questions, as well as permissible limitations. If the substantive content of a right is understood as having a minimum core and wider scope and is interpreted using the accepted and established concepts within article 2 and article 4, proportionality does not need to be engaged. In fact, such

[352] Young (n 333) 256.

[353] ibid 268.

[354] Alain Zysset and Antoinette Scherz, 'Proportionality as Procedure: Strengthening the Legitimate Authority of the UN Committee on Economic, Social and Cultural Rights' (2021) 10(3) *Global Constitutionalism* 524–46, 526.

[355] ibid 537.

[356] ibid 541.

an engagement would represent a breach of the fundamental requirement that under article 4 minimum core content cannot be limited under any circumstances (as it would limit the essence of the right).[357]

Under article 2(1) the position is less clear, owing to the lack of clarity regarding minimum core obligations and permissible retrogression.[358] It would in the minimum constitute non-compliance with minimum core obligations if they could justify proportional de facto limitations in line with the 'impossibility test' as set out in the Committee's Statement on Max Available Resources under the Optional Protocol and General Comment 3,

> 6. As regards the core obligations of States parties in relation to each of the Covenant rights, General Comment No. 3 states that, in order for a State party to be able to attribute its failure to meet its core obligations to a lack of available resources, it must demonstrate that every effort has been made to use all resources that are at its disposal in an effort to satisfy, as a matter of priority, those core obligations.[359]

At worst, it would constitute a violation of minimum core obligations if they could not pass this test. Moeckli argues that in the past the CESCR has been too disparate in their interpretation of the ICESCR and correlate obligations,

---

[357] See previous discussion in Chapters One and Two.

[358] See previous discussion in Chapter Two.

[359] UN Committee on Economic, Social and Cultural Rights, an Evaluation of the Obligation to Take Steps to the 'Maximum of Available Resources' Under an Optional Protocol to the Covenant, Statement (21 September 2007) E/C.12/2007/1, para. 6; CESCR, 'General Comment No. 3: The Nature of States Parties' Obligations (Art. 2, Para. 1 of the Covenant)', UN Doc E/1991/23 (14 December 1990), para. 9; see also Uprimny et al (n 16) 624–53.

oscillating between differing methods of interpretation causing both inconsistency in interpretation but also being detrimental to their legitimacy. The example of the recent application of proportionality and reasonableness to the minimum core as opposed to the previous inviolability of the minimum core illustrates this inconsistency.[360] Ultimately, it is contended that no limitations are permitted upon the minimum core of ESCRs, as this is in direct breach of the triple test as set out in article 4, and in light of the purpose of the limitations clause as evident from the *travaux préparatoires*. Thus, no proportionality analysis is engaged in relation to the minimum core content of a right.

Another key occurrence that has influenced the development of the Committee's reasonableness review generally, and in relation to article 4, has been the advent of the Optional Protocol to the ICESCR.[361] As Grohmann notes, this 'opens up the possibility to interpret Covenant provisions in a thorough manner'.[362] Article 8(4) of the Optional Protocol provides:

> When examining communications under the present Protocol, the Committee shall consider the *reasonableness* of the steps taken by the State Party in accordance with part II of the Covenant. In doing so, the Committee shall bear in mind that the State Party may adopt a range of

[360] Zysset and Scherz (n 354) 530; Daniel Moeckli, 'Interpretation of the ICESCR: Between Morality and State Consent' in Helen Keller, Daniel Moeckli and Corina Heri (eds), *The Human Rights Covenants at 50: Their Past, Present, and Future* (OUP 2018) 65.

[361] Optional Protocol to the International Covenant on Economic, Social and Cultural Rights, 2008, United Nations Treaty Series, vol. 2922, p 29. Doc. A/63/435. Entry into Force 5 May 2013, Signatories: 46. Parties: 29.

[362] Grohmann (n 256) Abstract, 1.

> possible policy measures for the implementation of the rights set forth in the Covenant.[363]

The Committee have developed a number of criteria for assessing reasonableness within the individual communications procedure: In their Statement on Maximum Available Resources under the Optional Protocol they state:

> 8. In considering a communication concerning an alleged failure of a State party to take steps to the maximum of available resources, the Committee will examine the measures that the State party has effectively taken, legislative or otherwise. In assessing, whether they are 'adequate' or '*reasonable*', the Committee may take into account, *inter alia*, the following considerations:
>
> (a) The extent to which the measures taken were deliberate, concrete and targeted towards the fulfilment of economic, social and cultural rights;
> (b) Whether the State party exercised its discretion in a non-discriminatory and non-arbitrary manner;
> (c) Whether the State party's decision (not) to allocate available resources was in accordance with international human rights standards;
> (d) Where several policy options are available, *whether the State party adopted the option that least restricts Covenant rights;*
> (e) The time frame in which the steps were taken;
> (f) Whether the steps had taken into account the precarious situation of disadvantaged and marginalized individuals or groups and, whether they were

[363] Article 8(4) Optional Protocol to the International Covenant on Economic, Social and Cultural Rights, 2008. Emphasis added.

> non-discriminatory, and whether they prioritized grave situations or situations of risk.[364]

Thus, the reasonableness test includes a strong vulnerability assessment, based on the principle of non-discrimination and akin to that found in the South African Constitutional Courts practice, for example in *Grootboom*.[365] It also includes an article 2 resources assessment; a temporal aspect as per usual limitations criteria and a proportionality assessment, that is, section 8 (d) requiring the least restrictive options. On face value, the test appears to be concerned more with article 2(1) concepts as opposed to article 4. The only reference to limitations is implicit within provision 8 (d) where states need to demonstrate they have utilised the least restrictive policy possible when restricting rights, and the reference to temporality. However, if read collectively, the Statement reflects the combination of reasonableness and proportionality theorised by Young. Additionally, this Statement illustrates the nexus between article 4 limitations and article 2(1) concepts such as progressive realisation and non-retrogression.[366]

Liebenberg argues that:

> The Committee has developed sound admissibility criteria, and a solid model of review to guide it in applying the reasonableness standard in Article 8(4) of the Optional Protocol. This jurisprudential approach has enabled the Committee to chart a skilful course thus

364 UN Committee on Economic, Social and Cultural Rights, an Evaluation of the Obligation to Take Steps to the 'Maximum of Available Resources' Under an Optional Protocol to The Covenant, Statement, E/C.12/2007/1 (21 September 2007), para. 8. Emphasis added.

365 *Grootboom*, 2001 (1) SA 46 (CC) paras 43–4.

366 Grohmann notes that 'The reasonableness review, […], is then closely connected to Article2(1) ICESCR and thus the principle of progressive realisation' (Grohmann (n 256) 4).

> far between sovereignty and accountability. This bodes well for strengthening the normative legitimacy of the Optional Protocol and advancing the broader project of the justiciability of economic, social, and cultural rights.[367]

Of course, the CESCR acting in their adjudicatory role under the Optional Protocol are not unusual in developing the criteria to be used in adjudication from that set out in the Covenant. However, it is important that the framework developed retains the ethos and intention of the article 4 clause itself. It is clear that in relation to individual communications under the Optional Protocol as borne out by the instrument itself and the practice of the Committee, that they have developed a reasonableness doctrine, which combines a reasonableness test with proportionality as a subset. As evidenced in Chapter Three, such a test has been applied to assess the lawfulness of limitations under the Covenant in relation to the right to housing. However, as reflected in the analysis of the jurisprudence of the Committee, 'the Committee is not consistent in referring explicitly to Article 4 of the Covenant (the limitations provision in the Covenant)'.[368] In sum, 'The coherence and rigor of the Committee's evolving jurisprudence under the Optional Protocol would benefit from greater clarity on the role of Article 4 in its legal analysis of communications.'[369] While Liebenberg correctly predicted that the 'criteria for guiding the application of the reasonableness standard' would evolve in future jurisprudence,[370] there are still several issues to be clarified. For example, it is unclear whether the minimum core is inviolable and as such whether it can be limited. While

367 Liebenberg (n 249) 48.

368 ibid 84.

369 ibid.

370 ibid.

article 4 would seem to clearly prohibit this, if article 2(1) is engaged instead, the confusion over the 'impossibility test' is raised. As noted by Grohmann, one important question that remains uncertain is how the 'developing proportionality analysis under the individual complaints procedure […] relates to or incorporates other ICESCR concepts, such as minimum core obligations'.[371] As Grohmann notes, 'all these principles and concepts, […] might influence, reinforce or even impair each other'.[372] Hence further research is required to fully understand the complex interactions between such concepts under the Covenant and the impact on the enjoyment of ESCRs on the ground.

Finally, it is important to highlight that this doctrine has developed specifically in response to individual communications. As such, outside of individual petition, for example in monitoring and assessment under the state periodic reporting procedure, the weighting of such analysis may be less relevant. In this context a broader reasonableness assessment might be required in relation to wider state policies and progressive realisation overall.[373]

4.4 Concluding remarks

The complexity of the legal framework of assessing permissible limitations under article 4 of ICESCR is evident. With

---

371 Grohmann (n 256) Abstract, 1.

372 ibid. See also Brian Griffey, 'The "Reasonableness" Test: Assessing Violations of State Obligations under the Optional Protocol to the International Covenant on Economic, Social and Cultural Rights' (2011) 11 *Human Rights Law Review* 275, 286–8; Joie Chowdhury, 'Unpacking the Minimum Core and Reasonableness Standards' in Jackie Dugard, Bruce Porter, Daniela Ikawa and Lilian Chenwi (eds), *Research Handbook on Economic, Social and Cultural Rights as Human Rights* (Edward Elgar 2020) 251, 254.

373 Grohmann (n 256) 4.

the advent of the Optional Protocol to the Covenant and the developing jurisprudence of the committee additional doctrines, particularly reasonableness and proportionality, have impacted upon the interpretation of limitations, supplementing the original triple test as set out in article 4. However, the wider applicability of these doctrines outside of individual petition is as yet untested. Moreover, it is not clear how such doctrines relate to existing doctrines under the ICESCR, most especially article 2(1) doctrines of progressive realisation, non-retrogression and maximum available resources. The scope of any reasonableness assessment is also of concern when engaging minimum core obligations. Consequently, the addition of these further requirements to the framework for assessing limitations under the Covenant may actually provide too much flexibility compounding the flexibility already provided for in article 2(1).

The following chapter considers how to develop a more consistent and clear limitations framework including a methodical and systematic legal test for the application of article 4.

FIVE

Moving Forwards: Developing a Clear and Consistent Limitations Framework Under The International Covenant on Economic, Social and Cultural Rights 1966

Having reviewed the doctrinal interpretation of article 4 under ICESCR, and surveyed and analysed the practice of the relevant UN human rights bodies, focussing most extensively the CESCR, as well as the practice of States Parties to the Covenant, it is evident that further clarity is required regarding the application of article 4 in situations of both crisis and normality.

The previous chapters have identified a number of issues that have resulted in problematic interpretation or indeed marginalisation of the use of article 4. These include the original lack of consensus around the scope and content of the provision, including concerns about the interaction with article 2(1) as set out in the *travaux préparatoires*; the continuing muddiness around the nexus between article 2(1) and article 4; and the move away from the original triple test as required by the ICESCR, to a perhaps overly complex legal test focused on the additional requirements of reasonableness and proportionality and heavily influenced by jurisprudential tools formulated for adjudication and implementation of civil and political rights.

Examining the experience of several crises, each of a differing nature, has also provided food for thought, enabling identification of both divergence in practice regarding limitations and commonalities in practice across different types of crises. It has also highlighted a lack of engagement around certain types of crises, for example, situations of armed conflict and wider conflict-affected settings.

In response to these findings, a number of recommendations are outlined with the aim of developing a clear and consistent limitations framework under the Covenant, thus assisting the CESCR in their work and providing States Parties with guidance as to when and how to engage article 4.

5.1 Clarity of scope and requirements

5.1.1 Clarifying the legal test

A clear and systematic legal test is required and should be applied with consistency when assessing the lawfulness of limitations. There is a need to clarify what standards should be used for reasoning and interpretation of article 4 and whether they should go beyond the triple test. As noted previously, the legal test is most developed when considering individual communications under the Optional Protocol to the ICESCR. As this is already in place, the Committee are not likely to regress on this methodology now. Consequently, moving forwards, the CESCR need to clarify how this approach will be consolidated within their jurisprudence, but more crucially how they will apply such principles more widely in their standard setting and monitoring process for States Parties. Should states be justifying their use of article 4 by reference to undertaking reasonableness or proportionality analysis or should they apply the triple test as provided under article 4? Lucidity is imperative for states to aid their reporting and compliance with obligations. Therefore, overall, the legal test requires clarity and a systematic and consistent approach.

It is contended that when assessing whether existing limitations on economic, social and cultural rights (ESCRs) are permissible, the CESCR should construct a two-stage test: Stage 1 is to begin with an explicit assessment of the limitations against the requirements of the original triple test. This must include consideration of the scope of the limitations in relation to the minimum core content/obligations of the right in question. This ensures conformity with the requirement that the 'essence' – the very nature of the right is protected (inviolable). Only once this has been undertaken should Stage 2, a substantive reasonableness assessment, be carried out. This reasonableness test is likely to include a proportionality assessment when assessing an individual petition.

5.1.2 Differentiating between article 4 and article 2(1) issues

In order to apply the legal test effectively, it is also crucial to establish whether existing de facto limitations on the enjoyment of ESCRs engage article 2(1) or whether they should actually be considered under article 4. This requires clarifying the nexus between article 2(1) and article 4, including consideration as to whether going forwards they should be read together (as advocated most recently by the CESCR) and/or indeed whether they need to be more clearly demarcated when considering reductions/restrictions in ESCRs enjoyment. It is contended that while they clearly require consideration in parallel, they are distinct provisions that require discrete analysis.[374] Article 2(1) should be reserved for assessing progress and a general *reduction* in the enjoyment of rights, whereas article 4 pertains to deliberate, formally declared, specific, time-limited *restrictions*. Unfortunately, the recent lack of clarity regarding the permissibility of retrogression and the conception of retrogressive measures as quasi -limitations has at times clouded this distinction.[375]

[374] Saul et al (n 78) 246.

[375] While outside the scope of this book, further research to definitively establish the exact nature and scope of the obligation of progressive realisation and the mirror opposite concept of retrogression under article

Moreover, this conceptual nexus between article 2(1) and article 4 is necessarily complex and cloudy, as all limitations on economic, social and cultural rights will raise questions of resources. Even when we consider the balancing of rights (as article 4 was originally intended to deal with), this is usually going to encroach on resource issues when we are dealing with ESCRs. Key differentials that can help in deciding whether something should be viewed as an article 2(1) issue or an article 4 issue include *temporality* and *intent*. Concerning *temporality*, if the measures taken are indicative of a general reduction in the enjoyment of ESCRs and therefore likely to be more permanent, they can be seen as more likely an issue of retrogression, but if they are a result of deliberate actions designed to tackle short-term issues then they are more likely to engage article 4.

The second key principle that should be considered is *intent*. As evidenced by the practice of the Committee in their standard setting and through jurisprudence, as well as in the states reports, de facto limitations caused by resource issues are often used by states as a reason for 'limiting' rights and article 2(1) is used by the Committee as a tool for assessing restrictions on the enjoyment of rights. The point here is that these restrictions are not declared as formal restrictions; rather they are a matter of fact (restrictions on the enjoyment of the rights in reality). However, states could and arguably do use the 'grey area' around retrogression to justify restrictions on the enjoyment of rights that should actually be overt and declared as formalised limitations under article 4. This is further complicated by the insistence that retrogressive measures must be deliberate.[376] It is contended that actually retrogression is more often by omission or neglect – a situation

2.1 is required. Subsequently, this will help to qualify the intersection of article 2(1) and article 4 and the application of article 4 moving forwards. For example, see Warwick (n 376).

[376] See Ben T.C. Warwick, 'Unwinding Retrogression: Examining the Practice of the Committee on Economic, Social and Cultural Rights'

where states have failed to put in place measures to address impacts, which then result in retrogression in the enjoyment of rights. Consequently, the idea of deliberate retrogression and intentional limitations on rights are brought into direct tension. Subsequently, it is argued that retrogression by omission should be recognised, and second, that if retrogressive measures are intentional, that is, deliberately designed to halt or cause a reduction in rights enjoyment, then they should be assessed to see if the state is actually putting in place a limitation on rights without declaring them as such.[377] In such situations, the Committee should insist on the formal engagement of article 4 to ensure increased scrutiny and review.

Lastly, given the questions over retrogressive measures and the possibility of non-compliance with the minimum core, clearly demarcating article 4 limitations will support the fundamental principle that the minimum core of rights cannot be lawfully limited, under any circumstances.[378] Moreover, while not requiring a formal state of emergency, indeed regardless of whether a particular context can be said to constitute an emergency, article 4 is likely to be applied in situations where the state is under some degree of abnormal pressure, whether that be due to political, economic or social factors and whether they arise from internal or external forces. In such situations

---

(2019) 19 *Human Rights Law Review* 467; Warwick (n 151) 256 for an analysis of retrogression.

[377] Such an assessment must also include asking questions as to individual impacts of retrogressive measures on vulnerable groups, for example, versus a general decline in enjoyment of ESCRs. See Sigrun Skogly, 'The Right to Continuous Improvement of Living Conditions and Human Rights of Future Generations: A Circle Impossible to Square?' in Jessie Hohmann and Beth Goldblatt (eds), *The Right to the Continuous Improvement of Living Conditions: Responding to Complex Global Challenges* (Hart Publishing 2021) 147–63.

[378] Clarifying the minimum core obligations of ESCRs in crisis situations will also be required if this has not been undertaken to date, for example in conflict affected situations.

whether the enjoyment of ESCRs is reduced (article 2.1) or restricted under article 4, additional or special measures may be necessary to protect the minimum core rights of the most vulnerable. This may entail a change of priorities or specific measures to ensure the delivery of the minimum core content of ESCRs. Thus the assessment of both article 2(1) and article 4 must include the requirement to protect the most vulnerable in society, as is already the practice of the CESCR.[379]

Ultimately, in the interpretation of article 4, the Committee must ensure that the developing legal framework does not result in extensive limitations to ESCRs due to the 'double flexibility' of combining original concepts from article 4 with more extensive standards of review for restrictions, such as reasonableness and proportionality, including by limiting minimum core of rights due to retrogression under article 2(1) and/or reasonableness review. The over burgeoning and complex tests under the Optional Protocol, in particular, will require careful and cautious review. Additionally, the impact of these additional principles on article 4 limitations more widely for example for State Reporting need to be considered.

5.1.3 Encourage the use of article 4 when necessary

In light of the previous discussion, it is also crucial to encourage states and the CESCR to utilise article 4 in practice. The empirical evidence has demonstrated that article 4 is not being utilised as much as it should be. Moving forwards, it is contended that a more robust, positive and forceful use of article 4 is required and beneficial. The Committee should

---

379 S.I. Skogly, 'The Right to Continuous Improvement of Living Conditions and Human Rights of Future Generations: A Circle Impossible to Square?' in Jessie Hohmann and Beth Goldblatt (eds), *The Right to the Continuous Improvement of Living Conditions: Responding to Complex Global Challenges* (Hart Publishing 2021) 147, 154; CESCR General Comment No. 3 (n 170) para. 11.

encourage states to formally engage article 4 if they believe states are de facto limiting rights through the 'back door'. When States Parties are struggling to realise the full scope of ESCRs, they should be encouraged to be open and transparent and seek permissible limitations under article 4. Only by encouraging states to engage this article, can the Committee monitor restrictions through the legal process set out under article 4, thus encouraging strict scrutiny and review. In this way, they can ensure restrictions are legitimate and in conformity with article 4 triple test.

5.2 Specificity – addressing each context and crisis

Relatedly, in order to clarify the scope and content of article 4 (and article 2(1)) it is important to be clear that article 4 applies in times of crisis but also in times of normality. Consequently, when article 4 is invoked or should be invoked, each specific context needs to be considered specifically as each situation will bring different challenges for the enjoyment of ESCRs. Moreover, the type of crisis, requires consideration, as at times different legal frameworks, for example, international humanitarian law may be applicable. Although there are commonalities in that all situations could result in resource issues and the need for limitations, it is also evident from the experience of past 'emergencies' that the challenges raised by an economic crisis, public health crisis or a situation of armed conflict, are all unique and have resulted in varying responses. In the case of economic crisis, the approach of the CESCR was more focused on article 2(1) issues, non-retrogression, resources and adopting an accommodation regime. In the case of the pandemic, it was more a question of balancing ESCRs with restrictions for the 'greater good' of society, although explicitly based on criteria lifted from the emergency regime under the ICCPR. Finally, in the case of conflict affected settings practice is yet to be determined. However, states practice would appear to demonstrate a strong leaning to equating conflict with states of emergency, civil and political rights emergency regimes. Crucially, States Parties appear unclear concerning states of exception and emergency and their obligations under the ICESCR. As such, the Committee need to clarify that article 4 applies in times of 'normality' and crisis. Further, they should ensure that the limitations regime they develop does not support such a 'state of exception' regime.

5.3 Authenticity and ethos

Finally, and particularly in response to the ever-greater lean towards a limitations regime closer to that of the ICCPR and of civil and political rights generally, it is argued that it is crucial to ensure a specific limitations regime, designed for ESCRs and incorporating the original concepts from the Covenant. While other scholars have argued for 'greater common ground in the legal standards for restrictions on both economic, social and cultural rights and civil and political rights',[380] it is contended that the opposite is required. While all human rights are interdependent, arguably developing an effective legal framework for limitations of economic and social rights under the ICESCR requires a distinct and unique legal regime, which reflects their unique nature as well as the specific doctrinal and conceptual framework of the ICESCR.

It is imperative to stay true to the ethos of the treaty itself and to the interpretation of the Covenants concepts and principles as intended in the *travaux*. As set out in the Vienna Convention on the Law of Treaties (1969) (VCLT)[381] article 31 General rule of interpretation, 'A treaty shall be interpreted in good

[380] Forman (n 84) 202.

[381] Vienna Convention on the Law of Treaties (VCLT), Vienna on 23 May 1969. Entered into force on 27 January 1980, United Nations Treaty Series, vol. 1155, p. 331.

faith in accordance with the ordinary meaning to be given to the terms of the treaty in their context and in the light of its object and purpose.'[382] Moreover, 'there shall be also taken into account [...] any subsequent practice in the application of the treaty which establishes the agreement of the parties regarding its interpretation'.[383] The practice of the CESCR including General Comments[384] as well as jurisprudence of the Committee can be considered authoritative interpretation of ICESCR including article 4. Consequently, it is crucial that the Committee develop a consistent and methodical legal test regarding article 4.

That is not to say that the CESCR cannot be progressive and develop the interpretation of the treaty (and the clause) over time. For example, further guidance can be taken from the Inter-American Court of Human Rights through its interpretative methodology based upon the *pro homine* or *pro personae* principle, meaning that human rights provisions should be interpreted with 'maximum benefit to the individual'.[385] The *pro personae* principle,

> informs all human rights law, by virtue of which one must resort to the most extensive interpretation of a fundamental right when enforcing such right; and, conversely, to the narrowest rule or interpretation when establishing permanent restrictions on the exercise of rights. This principle coincides with the

---

[382] VCLT 1969, Section 3. Interpretation of Treaties, Article 31 (1) General rule of interpretation. See also, article 31(2) and article 32 Supplementary means of interpretation.

[383] VCLT 1969, Section 3. Interpretation of Treaties, article 31 (3) (b).

[384] See Bueno de Mesquita et al (n 157) 4.

[385] Hayde Rodarte Berbera, 'The Pro Personae Principle and Its Application by Mexican Courts' (2017) 4(1) *Queen Mary Human Rights Law Review* 1–27, 9.

> fundamental feature of human rights law, namely, in favor of man.[386]

This principle as developed by the Court is founded on the VCLT article 31 in combination with article 29 of the American Convention on Human Rights, which provides Restrictions Regarding Interpretation.[387]

> According to this, human rights norms should be interpreted as extensively as possible when recognising individuals' rights and, by contrast, as restrictively as possible when the norm imposes limits on the enjoyment of human rights. At the same time, the principle commands that in case of conflicts between human rights norms, the norm that better protects the individual's rights should prevail.[388]

As Hayde argues, 'This *pro personae* methodology involves, in tandem with an evolutive approach, the maximisation of the object and purpose of human rights treaties.'[389] While this does not mean the text of the treaty can be ignored,[390] it does ensure the overarching aim of the treaty must be adequately considered.

---

[386] Pinto quoted in J. Contesse, 'Conventionality Control and the Limits of Pro Persona Jurisprudence' (2023) 3(1) *The Italian Review of International and Comparative Law* 121–32, 125.

[387] American Convention on Human Rights, 'Pact of San Jose, Costa Rica (B-32)' (1969), Entry Into Force: 07/18/78, OAS, Treaty Series, No. 36, 24 States Parties.

[388] Rodarte Berbera, (n 385) 9.

[389] ibid, 7.

[390] Birgit Schlütter, 'Aspects of Human Rights Interpretation by the UN Treaty Bodies' in Helen Keller and Geir Ulfstein (eds), *UN Human Rights Treaty Bodies: Law and Legitimacy* (CUP 2012) 280.

5.4 Recommendations for the CESCR

In addressing some of the weaknesses in the current practice regarding article 4, there are a number of measures that the CESCR could consider implementing: Most notably further development is required is in the application of article 4 requirements to the states periodic reporting procedure. There is a need to strengthen the scrutiny of a States Parties compliance with their obligations under article 4 of the Covenant, particularly in situations of crisis. As such, the Committee could amend their treaty specific reporting guidelines and call for an amendment to the general state reporting guidelines, to make it clear states should report on article 4 limitations to ICESCR, not just those under the ICCPR article 4 or in relation to civil and political rights at a domestic level. In addition, the revised follow-up procedure to the Optional Protocol,[391] together with the proposed introduction of a new 'eight-year predictable reporting cycle'[392] may enhance the ability of the CESCRs to consider article 4 limitations more effectively, for example allowing for more frequent review and monitoring of state compliance with individual and general recommendations within state periodic reporting sessions.

Second, the CESCR could draft a dedicated general comment or issue a Statement on limitations under the Covenant. Moreover, they could draft a General Comment or in the

[391] See Committee on Economic, Social and Cultural Rights: report on the 60th, 61st, 62nd sessions (20–24 February 2017, 29 May–23 June 2017, 18 September–6 October 2017), E/2018/22, E/C.12/2017/3, Annex II, Working Methods Concerning the Committee's Follow-up to Views Under the Optional Protocol to the International Covenant on Economic, Social and Cultural Rights, 61st session, 23 June 2017, pp 21–2.

[392] United Nations Committee on Economic, Social and Cultural Rights, Report on the seventy-fifth and seventy-sixth sessions (12 February–1 March and 9–27 September 2024), E/2025/22, E/C.12/2024/, United Nations: Geneva, 2025.

minimum a Statement on Permissible Limitations to assist States Parties in understanding their obligations, and the scope and basis for article 4 restrictions. This would contribute greatly to addressing the lack of understanding by States Parties.

More widely, the Committee could make certain they include a paragraph on the requirements of article 4 limitations within future general comments, noting how they may impact in specific contexts, for example in armed conflict or natural disasters or addressing their relevance to the specific right in question.

Lastly, they could develop a standard paragraph for Concluding Observations on permissible limitations, akin to the standard paragraph on the Sustainable Development Goals (SDGs) and development, developed since 2019.[393]

[393] See, for example, Committee on Economic, Social and Cultural Rights, Concluding observations on the fourth periodic report of Cameroon E/C.12/CMR/CO/4, 25 March 2019, para. 68 and Committee on Economic, Social and Cultural Rights, Concluding Observations on the Fifth Periodic Report of Iraq. E/C.12/IRQ/CO/5, 14 March 2024, para. 60, and the Concluding observations on the second periodic report of Indonesia E/C.12/IDN/CO/2, para. 66.

Conclusion

'Like all other legal rules, norms recognizing or conferring rights or imposing limitations on them are subject to a continuing process of interpretation.'[394] This book has attempted to contribute to that process of interpretation by providing an overview of theory and practice of rules concerning permissible limitations under article 4 of the ICESCR to date. However, this is the beginning of the conversation on article 4 and the interpretation of permissible limitations under the Covenant must continue to evolve.

By identifying and analysing the shortcomings in theory and practice to date, a number of key proposals have been suggested to progress the understanding of the scope and application of article 4. These include recommendations to provide clarity of scope and develop a clear and consistent legal test; to ensure specificity in approach as regards the context and crisis and to embrace authenticity to the Covenant principles itself, supporting a specific approach to ESCRs limitations rather than a general limitations approach which attempts to mirror CPRs treaties and jurisprudence. Due to the unique nature of ESCRs, this is crucial.

To conclude, in the current global climate where economic, social and cultural rights are already extensively violated, both in times of normality and in crisis, a specific approach to limitations on ESCRs is required. A general approach to limitations is not appropriate due to nature of the rights in question (often basic needs necessary for survival) and the existing flexibility provided in the general obligations within

[394] Daes (n 20) p. 112, para. 125.

the ICESCR (notably progressive realisation; minimum core). Moreover, the wording of article 4 is unequivocal, with only one legitimate reason for restricting such rights – promoting the general welfare of society. The more stringent and truer the basis is on which states can limit the enjoyment of economic, social and cultural rights, the better for the implementation and enjoyment of economic, social and cultural rights in times of crisis and times of normality.

Index

References to footnotes show both the page number and the note number (26n91).

H

I

Q

R

S

T